LIVING IN LOVE

How to Create a Lifestyle of Love, Faith, Bliss, and Crazy-Ass Manifesting (All in Thirty-One Days)

Colinda Latour

BALBOA.PRESS
A DIVISION OF HAY HOUSE

Copyright © 2023 Colinda Latour.

All rights reserved. No part of this book may be used or reproduced by any means, graphic, electronic, or mechanical, including photocopying, recording, taping or by any information storage retrieval system without the written permission of the author except in the case of brief quotations embodied in critical articles and reviews.

Balboa Press books may be ordered through booksellers or by contacting:

Balboa Press
A Division of Hay House
1663 Liberty Drive
Bloomington, IN 47403
www.balboapress.com
844-682-1282

Because of the dynamic nature of the Internet, any web addresses or links contained in this book may have changed since publication and may no longer be valid. The views expressed in this work are solely those of the author and do not necessarily reflect the views of the publisher, and the publisher hereby disclaims any responsibility for them.

The author of this book does not dispense medical advice or prescribe the use of any technique as a form of treatment for physical, emotional, or medical problems without the advice of a physician, either directly or indirectly. The intent of the author is only to offer information of a general nature to help you in your quest for emotional and spiritual well-being. In the event you use any of the information in this book for yourself, which is your constitutional right, the author and the publisher assume no responsibility for your actions.

Interior Image Credit: Rachael Holmes Photography

Print information available on the last page.

ISBN: 979-8-7652-3932-2 (sc)
ISBN: 979-8-7652-3934-6 (hc)
ISBN: 979-8-7652-3933-9 (e)

Library of Congress Control Number: 2023905720

Balboa Press rev. date: 03/27/2023

To my mum, one of my greatest teachers
1935–2022

Contents

Acknowledgements ix
Introduction...xi

Part One: A Love Story

Chapter 1: When My Face Met the Pole 1
Chapter 2: Creating an Inner Monologue You
             Want to Hear..11
Chapter 3: Throw Your Head Back and Say, "I Quit!"....23
Chapter 4: Your New Story is Yours to Create 34
Chapter 5: Becoming Love..49
Chapter 6: The Divine Omnipresence that is Love 63
Chapter 7: When Mishaps Come Calling.........................78

Part Two: A Love Toolbox

Chapter 8: Doing Love is the Way to Go..........................89
Chapter 9: Now is the Time to Do Love 108
Chapter 10: Raw Results and Lavish Love....................118

Afterword: Becoming a Global Love Generator.............133
Appendix I: Statistics and Insights................................135
Appendix II: Love Action Matrix and Checklist............157

Acknowledgements

This book has been in the works my entire life. It started with the first story I told myself about love and carried on from there. I would like to thank my friends, family, and everyone who has supported me on this journey. Your encouragement kept me going. A special thank you to Colin Thorpe and Rhonda Howells for being my beta readers.

Introduction

Solving the world's problems with the simple notion of love seems far too flippant or cavalier, but when you create an environment of love that surrounds your daily life, it doesn't seem too far-fetched. However, before I arrived at a point where I believed this, I had to work my way through a maze of emotions that ultimately led me to becoming the love-filled being we are all meant to be.

During childhood, I'd find myself cowering in my bedroom whenever there was a fight in my home. Knees curled up around my chest with my hands over my ears, gently rocking, I'd whisper into the air, "Please make it stop, please make it stop."

As an adult, whenever I took the time to contemplate the state of our world, I'd often find myself doing the same. I'd catch a glimpse of a headline, have a discussion with a friend, or listen to a podcast that offered ways to get through *these difficult times*, and I'd lament over why we can't just live in peace and be kind and thoughtful to one another. The negativity was too difficult to handle.

I grew up in fear and rage, and now they seemed to be commonplace in our world. I wanted those emotions out of my life and no longer running the show. I needed to find a way to do it and create my own solution.

So, I did.

This solution came to me at a difficult time. My sister had passed away, and the world was dealing with COVID. I could not fly home and join my family to grieve, and I needed to do something that would make me feel better.

I had no idea that what I came up with would work so effectively, nor did I expect it to escalate from seeking internal peace and love to something much bigger than myself. When I recognised the potential of what I created, I knew I had to share it. I was elated and wanted to shout my discovery from the proverbial mountaintop: *Simple acts of love will change the world!*

If you're thinking to yourself, "Sure, love will change the world … but I already do things I love, and I haven't noticed much difference. I certainly haven't stopped any wars or ended global warming."

I get it.

But based on the solution I created, in the form of a thirty-one-day challenge, I have discovered that consciously performing daily acts of love towards yourself and others (on top of the normal displays of affection and utterances of "I love you" to the special people in your life) will change your reality and the world around you. The love that is generated through these *love actions* will only expand; it has to.

I am sure you have seen an example of this. If you hug your child, pet, or partner, more often than not, they return that affection. Now, imagine love being created simply by putting love into your activities and thoughts throughout the day. This will create an environment surrounded with love—and eventually, if enough people live this way, we can create a love-filled world.

This does take some focus and work at first, because we're not taught to put love into our daily actions, such as when doing the dishes or communicating with our colleagues. Instead, we're taught to focus on getting up in the morning, going to school or work, doing well, getting paid, shopping, eating, watching television, walking the dog, talking to family and friends, and getting a good night's sleep. Repeat. We live on autopilot, and that is all right. We are creatures of habit. But what I want to introduce is living on autopilot from love. I want love to be humanity's go-to way of existing.

Think of something you love. Now, really concentrate on how wonderful it makes you feel. Next, contemplate feeling like that most of the time, like your life is a warm embrace. Think about how this would impact the people you interact with and the places you go. If even a small percentage of the population decided to live in this close-to-constant loving state, it would have a far-reaching influence. People would be going about their lives in a kinder, gentler fashion.

Wherever you are on your path of love—be it self-love, familial, romantic, or any form of love—I invite you to read these pages and introduce yourself to a new way of living; a way of life where love is at the forefront of all your actions, thoughts, words, and gestures; a way of life where you don't even have to think about it. You are just love, the very state we are meant to be.

If I have piqued your interest and you are wondering, "How do I do this? How do I reach and maintain a loving attitude when there is so much *not love* in the world?"

Easy.

Take the Full-On Love Challenge or one of the mini-challenges in this book.

I created these because I wanted that for myself—a life of love. What resulted was beyond any hopes and expectations. In only thirty-one days, I achieved a true sense of belonging and wholeness, finally feeling that connection and oneness we so often hear about. My faith that life was always working out for the best shot through the roof and remains unwavering, and now I frequently float through my days in bliss. These are only a few of the positive side effects of living in love.

Will my challenges change the world immediately? No. Will they change your world immediately? Yes!

And if enough people have the courage to stay with this new way of living we will change the world together.

Take a chance, flip the pages, and see what simple acts of love can do for you.

Part One

A Love Story

Tales from a very bumpy path of discovering self-love and, ultimately, divine love. Throw in some revelations, romance, and mishaps along the way.

Chapter 1

When My Face Met the Pole

I struggled with love throughout my life. I was constantly striving to receive it from someone else or give it away rather than keeping any of it for myself. I longed for feelings of affection and the unconditional care that is so often equated with love. Instead, from infanthood to adulthood, feelings of unworthiness simmered and kept me questioning, *Am I even loveable?*

This doubt manifested into a stream of unkind sentiments that ran on repeat in my head: *Did I behave well enough? Will my mum love me if I do this or that? Was I cool enough in high school? Am I pretty/smart/funny enough for a guy to ever love me? Am I working hard enough at work?*

All of these thoughts and thousands more droned on for years, perpetuating my loveless tale. But I was blind to the damage these thoughts were causing. I never considered that perhaps what I was putting into my head was what would present itself as reality. It all makes sense now, but it certainly didn't register at the time. Sadly, it took a literal shake-up for me to stop in my tracks and begin foraging for a new way of life—one where I began to show myself the love I so desperately sought from outside.

It was in London on a dank, cold December evening. I was on the train coming home from dinner with a friend, enslaved by a news story on my phone. I found this story particularly interesting, as it was about Turkey, and I had just moved from Istanbul months earlier. I couldn't take my eyes from what I was reading, not even for a moment.

I was like this for many years, gobbling up news stories, always needing to know the latest news. I was addicted and never missed a beat when it came to subjects that interested me. I was fuelled by a false belief that I needed to know everything in the world and keep up with current affairs. It did not matter what medium—I consumed it! I was oblivious to how bombarding myself with the negative energy of world events was affecting me.

That evening was no different. I was so entranced with the story, I kept reading it on my walk home. There I was, phone to face all the way from the train to the platform and then to the pavement. About halfway home, still deeply immersed in the lies and corruption detailed in the article, I did not see what was right in front of me. And that is when it happened.

Whack!

Head first, straight into a gritty square metal pole, so hard my body jolted.

Shocked, I shook my head in embarrassment and had a quick look around to see if anyone had witnessed my humiliating mishap. Thankfully, no one was there. Barely skipping a beat, and not really bothering to think about what had happened, I put the phone to my face again and kept reading as I continued my walk. A half block later, I felt something warm slip down my forehead. Curious, I touched it.

Blood. Damn.

I traced my fingertip up the blood trail to where I felt a ping-pong ball–sized lump. It was a doozy. At that point, I put my phone in my pocket and thought to myself, *Perhaps it's best to look where I am going.* It was those simple words

(OK, *and* the massive bump!) that put my mind into action and my life's trajectory on a diversion.

When I arrived home, I looked in the mirror and was stunned at how immense the bump was. I couldn't believe that my skin was able to stretch over this newly formed growth. I pitifully slumped into the bathroom and gently washed the now crusty brown blood from my forehead. I stared into my eyes as I rinsed the face cloth and didn't like what I was seeing—melancholy and dissatisfaction. I continued to look as I braced my hands on the sink and searched my pupils for the missing bits of my life I was only now sensing. The crash jarred my body and woke up my soul. Something was shifting inside. Holding my gaze, I asked my reflection, *What's missing? What am I seeking?*

Create a life you love

Staring back as I brushed my fingers across the colossal hill on my forehead, I had an epiphany. It was time I put more thought and effort into loving myself and not worrying about finding love elsewhere. I wanted to create a life I loved, no matter what transpired and even if I was the only one who could make that happen.

I don't know why, but I immediately knew I had to change what I was allowing into my consciousness. It was appropriately like a newsflash: *Colinda, stop with the news!* I laughed at the absurdity of receiving what seemed like a news bulletin about my obsession with the news and how it was not healthy. I was so addicted to it that every morning when I got up, I would roll out my yoga mat, open my laptop, and turn on one of my favourite news sources. I'd catch up on all the horrible things happening around the world while saluting the glorious sun shining through my window.

Looking back, I cannot imagine why I thought those two activities were a good match. Take it from me: yoga and news should never be combined. They just don't mesh.

Walking from the bathroom to my bedroom, I decided right then and there that this bad habit had to end. My relentless pursuit of what 90 per cent of the time was horrible in the world was not serving me. I needed to focus on good. I sat softly on my bed considering my decision while I nursed my wound and my dignity, feeling this shift continue.

Something inside me was coming alive. I had a yearning to improve, to focus on myself, and to change how I felt, spoke, and acted towards myself. I could feel discomfort rising as I went further with my introspection and started to think about other things I was doing that were not conducive to a life I loved. I pondered all the dates I had gone on and how not one so far had resulted in the life of love I craved. It was that line of thinking and finally the recognition that I was foolishly looking for love in all the wrong places that sowed the kernel of self-love I so desperately needed. The inkling of an idea that perhaps I should make myself the centre of love and not yearn for love from someone else started to blossom.

The night did not end there. In fact, it continued with further thought and heart-opening realizations. I was fed up with feeling unloved and blaming it on someone else. It was time I took control of my emotions and stopped letting my previous experiences with love continue to influence my reality.

Up until that evening, the proof I kept generating was that love received from others was littered with conditions and not reliable. Emotions given or presented to us from another person are out of our control, and we shouldn't depend on them to make us feel good, yet that is exactly what I was doing. I needed to get out of the head-and-heart space of relying on others and believe that *my love* was enough. It was reliable, and I could depend on it wholeheartedly. This night pushed me over the brink of letting life live me, and I started to take control, beginning with how I felt.

Up until that night, I had dabbled in self-development but never made a concerted effort to integrate it fully into my life. Instead, I allowed feelings of unworthiness and a "why me?" victim mentality to drive my life. Sure, I made plans and even updated them yearly on my birthday, but for the most part, life seemed to fall into my lap, and I didn't take responsibility for it.

Don't get me wrong: the life I was living was pretty darn good. But I still was searching for someone to complete it and fill it with love. When that didn't work, I went back to playing the victim and blaming my discontent on the failed relationship.

That whack to the head sent my life spinning and made me realize I was living a lie. I didn't need anyone to feel love or to make my life complete. I just didn't know it yet—how to achieve that level of confidence and self-love on my own. I was still too reliant on my old way of thinking: *Validate me or I don't matter.*

I sat on my bed trying to force ideas to flow about how to move away from this outside reliance and what I could do to strengthen my belief in myself. The more I tried to force things, though, the more difficult it became. I sat back exasperated and touched the bump on my forehead for a reminder of how quickly things can change. One moment I was essentially sleepwalking home, and the next I violently woke myself up.

Now, maybe it was time to stay awake and be more conscious of what I was putting into my head: no more news, no more waiting for life to happen to me. It was time to create my own life, one that I was elated to live and was filled with love. I smiled at that thought and felt the twinkling of power returning to my being.

I closed my eyes and took a few deep breaths, digesting all that had transpired since the short walk from the train station to my home. As I calmed, the question *How do I do this?* came to me, and just as clearly also came the answer.

The answer was *meditate*.

My eyes snapped open with that response, and my smile grew. I closed my eyes again and took a few more deep breaths, letting the peacefulness seep into my veins. This was what I was hoping for: the answers to start flowing and a path to a life of love to unfold.

I pulled my legs into a cross-legged seat and leaned against the wall at the head of my bed. My hands, palms up, instinctively curled into the thumb and pointer fingers gently touching as they rested on my thighs. Serenely, the words *Go inside, take the time to get to know your true self, find out who you really are, and get to know the loving being you are meant to be* floated behind my lids. I listened to my newfound inner voice and knew that this night had changed my life. It was time for a new adventure to begin, and it would start with self-love, something that was completely unfamiliar to me at the time.

That night was the beginning of a new life—so much so that I started referring to my life as having two parts, *pre-pole* and *post-pole*. Not looking where I was going that evening had propelled me into a life of love that started with healing my own heart and soul, then progressed into finding a love so pure and encompassing, I can only call it *divine love*. It is the love I yearned for but thought I would find in the arms of a partner or family member. Instead, I found it within myself. I find this very exciting, because it is always available, and now I know how to turn it on so it flows nonstop into my life.

This love did not come right away. It took time to undo all the hardwired feelings of unworthiness and fear that stubbornly seeped (and still do from time to time) into my heart. But it did come, and I am forever grateful for every step along my path that led me there. I hope that this book will help you on your own journey and perhaps lead you to this loving state sooner than me.

What is divine love?

For me, *divine love* is what some would call *God* and I call *Source* or *Source energy*. It is a higher consciousness that we are a part of and can feel when we are in such elevated emotional states as joy, bliss, peace, and love. It is within us and is the very essence of who we are and what connects us all. Divine love guides our intuition or inner voice and is the life force that created the miracle of our universe, planets, and all the creatures that exist in and outside our realm of consciousness.

Throughout this book, I will refer to *Source, Source energy, divine love,* or *love* interchangeably, because for me they are the same. If you do not believe in a God or a greater/higher consciousness, that is fine. We are all entitled to our beliefs, and I hope that my belief in Source and how we are part of Source energy does not dissuade you from continuing with this book. The power of love does not need you to believe in a higher consciousness because it *is* a higher consciousness.

So, how do we gain access to this love that is all around? How do we open our hearts to it and let it flow through our lives? How do we cease relying on others to make us feel loved, but rather rely on ourselves and faith so that we are constantly engulfed in love?

First, we make the decision to love ourselves and do whatever it takes to accept that we are whole, worthy, and loveable. Then, we take responsibility for our lives and work at creating a life we love.

Meditation is a gift of love

Meditation was where I began. I listened to my higher self that night and started meditating immediately. In fact, from that night onward, I meditated daily. It almost felt like I had no choice. When my intuition said to go inside and meditate, it was more than a suggestion; it was a command from a place of love I could not ignore.

I had flirted with meditation over the years. I studied it in my yoga learnings and attended a few classes, but I never made it a habit. Now it is so ingrained in my psyche that I rarely miss a day—and if I do, I feel it. I feel off-kilter, like something is missing. Meditation is the biggest gift of self-love I've ever given myself, and it is featured in my love challenge, which you will learn about in Chapter 5.

Diving in head first, I tried any type of meditation I came across or knew of already. It felt so good. I couldn't resist experimenting and researching the different methods and benefits. I tried all sorts and took note of the types I enjoyed the most or that brought me greater peace of mind. I played with what time of day worked best for me, or sometimes I'd have music, no music, talking, no talking, moving, sitting, lying down, chanting ... If I found a type of meditation that enticed me, I tried it. It became my new addiction: no more negative news, only positive peace!

There are so many different kinds of meditation to choose from that I think it is important for people to experiment and find the method that best suits them. It can be anything from staring into a flame to repeating a mantra. It can be walking through nature or sitting silently and still for hours or even minutes. It can be listening to someone on YouTube or a meditation app who talks you through certain subjects and helps you release pain or bring peace to your mind. It can be sending kindness and love to others, or simply quietly contemplating a problem with a different perspective.

Meditation is all of these things and so much more. For me, it is what calms my mind and my body and puts me in touch with Source. I tap into the loving energy field that we are all part of (everything is energy) and sometimes arrive at that place where I, as Colinda, no longer exist. I just am.

I didn't achieve that immediately, nor does it come frequently, but I did quickly notice improvements once meditation was part of my routine. I became calmer and more dedicated to improving myself. I was focused, slept better, felt less stressed, and cherished the exercise of taking quiet time for me. I had never considered the notion that essentially doing nothing would make me feel so wonderful. At the beginning, it helped immensely in getting me to a place in my life where I allowed myself to have the space and time to be quiet, appreciate life, and not feel guilty about it.

A few months after I began my regular practice, I settled into a routine of meditating as soon as I woke up. I lie cosily in bed with my headphones on, listening to a guided meditation that I choose each morning. Sometimes I do the same meditation for weeks. Other times, I switch it up. It all depends on how I feel and what my intentions are for the day.

During the first year, I often meditated multiple times a day (still do!) because I loved how it made me feel. Or sometimes, something would come up, and my inner guide would say, *Meditate on it.* If I received that message, I made a point of quietly pondering the issue with a fresh, calm mind. I would sit for ten to fifteen minutes, take a few deep breaths to relax myself, then set the intention for the solution or answer to present itself to me. When I listened to that inner voice and followed the guidance that came, I always felt like I made the right decision. In fact, listening to that voice the night my face met the pole is exactly why I started meditating and began my beautiful journey of love and self-discovery.

If you do not meditate, I highly recommend giving it a try. I cannot promote it enough. (I provide further information and guidance on meditating in Part Two, Chapter 8.) It is so powerful you can reap the rewards of feeling calmer and happier from only a few moments.

If you're scratching your chin or wondering, "How will I fit one more activity into my crammed diary?" don't fret—you don't need to meditate for long periods of time to make it worthwhile. At first, try it for even a minute or two and give yourself the gift of love by taking a few moments of stillness. Trust me, you will make time when you start to feel its benefits.

The biggest takeaway from my fateful pole-walking incident was the tiny seed of self-love that I planted and the gift of my first love action,[1] meditation, which gave me my first glimpse into creating a life of love. If I can give you, the reader, anything from this chapter, it would be not to wait until your face has a collision to get the love ball rolling. Just do it. You're worth it.

---

[1] I originally came up with the phrase *love action* for the actions I completed during my thirty-one-day challenge, the Full-On Love Challenge, but I will use it throughout the book to indicate tools and activities that create love in our lives.

Chapter 2

Creating an Inner Monologue You Want to Hear

Have you ever sat and listened to your inner monologue? I certainly never wanted to or took much notice of it until I decided to create a love-filled life. When I did start paying attention to what my brain was conjuring up, I knew it wasn't conducive to the life I wanted.

It is suggested that we think approximately 60,000 to 70,000 thoughts a day. Most of them, we are not even conscious of, or they are running on a loop that is so ingrained into our subconscious that we can't even tell they are there. I don't know about you, but for me, I wanted to make sure that the majority of those thoughts were positive—and that was before I realised the impact our thinking has on our reality.

I began to pay attention to my inner monologue and would try to catch any negative chatter as soon as I noticed it. Problem was, I didn't know what to replace those negative thoughts and beliefs with. I hadn't figured out yet that leaving a null value wasn't a solution. Being more aware was the first step. Next, I had to figure out how to retrain my brain not only to remove the negative thinking and limiting beliefs but to create new thoughts and beliefs as well as ones that served me on my journey.

It was the day after hitting my head that I found the first method for filling my consciousness with positivity. I had never even considered doing such a thing, but after the previous night's introspection and decision, I was open to anything that would help turn my life from loveless to love-*full*.

The next day, when I went to work, several people suggested (strongly) that I go to the hospital to see if I was concussed, and then go home and rest. I took their advice and walked to the accident and emergency ward at the nearest hospital. I happily learnt I did not have a concussion. I was just shaken up a bit, but the bump would slowly go down, and there would be no issues.

On my way home, I began to think about all I had done in my life, despite having coasted for the majority of it. As the list grew, I started feeling really proud. When I arrived at home, I hastily wrote my mental list of things I had accomplished in my journal, and after only a few moments, I was surprised by how much space I had filled. I loved it!

At that point, I decided to keep it as a living document and add to it whenever I accomplished new feats. I had never taken the time to really appreciate the effort, tenacity, and skills it took to reach all those goals and milestones, and seeing them on paper was a massive boost for me. It was the first time I truly recognised all my accomplishments. I had been proud of myself in the past, but never to the extent where I was blown away by all the things I had done merely by setting my mind to something and following through.

Journal of self-appreciation

I call this my *Journal of Self-Appreciation and Self-Worth*, and it is now a couple of volumes. I love going back through the pages, re-reading the entries, and adding more as time goes on. It's a great reminder of some of the reasons why I should love myself.

If you are having difficulty recognising your accomplishments, you are being too hard on yourself. You learnt to walk, you learnt to talk, you can read, you dressed yourself, you may have even made your bed today. Write any accomplishment, no matter how small, if you are finding it hard to start.

Please don't think it's vain or egotistical to do such an exercise. It is important to give yourself a pat on the back—it is part of loving yourself. Ironically, we are our harshest critics, but if we could accept and love ourselves, we would be much happier and would find it easier to love and accept others as well. It is time to love all that we are and *all* that we've done.

After I re-read my initial list, I noticed how good I felt. It was like I was radiating pure positivity, and I made the choice to find more things that helped me feel this way. I was amazed that once I set this intention, all the right things started to show up. I was guided to all the right books, podcasts, webinars, courses, and conferences. It was a barrage of information that kept coming, and when these gifts kept presenting themselves to me, I started to ruminate on the power of our thoughts.

How was I bringing things into my life simply by focusing on them? This curiosity drove me into the world of the law of attraction. As I learnt about that, I absorbed all that I could and did my best to apply it in my life regularly.

For those of you who are unfamiliar with the law of attraction, a simple way to explain it is that like attracts like. This is impacted not only by our words and thoughts but by our emotions and energy too. When we think about something we want (or something we don't want), what we focus on eventually becomes our reality. It's hard to swallow if you are sitting in debt, miserable, sad, or with feelings of lack, but when you break it down and analyse your thoughts and then measure them against your outside world, what do you see?

I saw a direct correlation between my life and my thinking and the words I spoke mentally or out loud. That was when I understood the power of our thoughts and words. I decided I needed more help and asked the universe for a new way to sweep my head clean of negative beliefs and thought patterns that did not serve me. A few days later, I was listening to a talk about the power we have to change our lives and was introduced to *affirmations*.

The gift of affirmations

I fell in love with affirmations from the moment I started using them. I noticed an immediate difference when I started to repeat positive phrases in words, consciously minding the thoughts that streamed through my head. I noticed a significant change in my demeanour and even in how I felt physically. I had more energy, felt lighter, and had a more positive outlook. I smiled more and felt an increased state of well-being.

As these positive feelings continued, my awareness cemented my belief that our thoughts and feelings affect our reality, and that what we put into the world with these thoughts and beliefs is exactly what we get back. I was buzzing with happiness and felt like I was exuding a happy energy all around me. I was vibrating with positivity!

When I speak of *vibrations* we exude, I am referring to the fact that we are energy, and as energy, we emanate frequencies. These frequencies are not only influenced by your physical self, which in fact is just vibrating energy particles, but also by your thoughts and feelings. When you are feeling depressed, people around you can *feel* it, same as when you are ecstatic and the energy radiating off you *feels* happy. The famous equation attributed to Einstein, $E = mc^2$, essentially states that mass and energy are interchangeable, that they are different forms of the same thing. Therefore, there is no doubt that we vibrate and produce different frequencies. These vibrations are broadcast into our body and surroundings, influencing the environment around us.

This became very apparent to me after I introduced affirmations into my daily practice and noticed a dramatic change in how complete strangers acted towards me whilst I repeated certain mantras. It was one of my favourite affirmations that provided evidence I could not ignore. One of the first affirmations I started repeating regularly was the statement, *I am love, I am peace, I am light and gratitude.* I chose those words to keep my thoughts focused on the state I wanted to exist in. Eventually, it naturally shortened to *I am love, I am light,* and I still repeat these words daily, eight years later.

At the time, I wrote the words on pieces of paper and put them on my mirror, on my walls, and in my wallet. I tried to make them my go-to thoughts. As those words repeatedly passed through my consciousness, they put me in a loving, joyful state. I walked around with a smile on my face and a skip to my step.

One day, shortly after I made this affirmation a habit, I was walking around the shops on a lunch break and noticed that several people I encountered smiled at me or said hello for no reason. I thought it was odd, as in London, people aren't usually overtly friendly to strangers. I kept track of how often and when I encountered this, and over the next few days, what I noticed was that when I was repeating those words mentally, people paid attention to me—they smiled at me or greeted me. When I wasn't repeating the mantra, they didn't.

I was pleasantly flabbergasted and excited at the same time. I know it was because those words were swirling in my head, embedding themselves in my consciousness and projecting a vibrant, happy energy to people passing by. People felt it and responded with the same energy. I was giddy with this social experiment I hadn't even planned and incredibly grateful for the life lesson that presented itself to me so beautifully. I could not have asked for better proof for my new knowledge.

What makes affirmations so powerful?

I believe it is the repetition that helps to recreate our thoughts and beliefs—plus, the emotions we attach to those words we repeat. Think of it: If you are repeating negative phrases such as *I'm not good enough, I'm stupid,* or *I'm not worthy of love, friends, abundance* ... you feel miserable. Whereas, if you are repeating wonderful statements like *I can do anything, I am loveable,* or *I am worthy,* the emotions that naturally attach themselves to those phrases are more genial. They make you feel good.

That is why, when studying affirmations, you will find several teachers suggesting you say them in the present tense. Introduce them with something to evoke a positive, happy emotion, and/or use "I am" to state them as a fact. They can be repeated multiple times in a row, throughout the day, or simply as a single statement. They are meant to affirm something you want to achieve, receive, or become.

You can choose to write them down as a regular practice or just once and put them in a place where you can read them often, as I did by putting them in my wallet and on my walls. I always have affirmations scattered throughout my house that I repeat when I notice them.

Affirmations can be long, short, or anywhere in between. The important bit is that they mean something to you, and you resonate with what they are saying. If you can't think of any, use other people's affirmations that you hear or read. I do both.

As mentioned, say them in the present as if what you are stating is already the case, and use a gratitude statement within the affirmation that will boost your emotion. If you say, "I will have ..." or "I am going to ..." or "I will feel ...," those statements are not affirming that you feel that way or you have something already. Rather, they are confirming that you do *not* have what you wish for. An "I am" statement sends a powerful message to your brain and into the universe that whatever you are affirming already exists, and you are declaring it to be fact.

I am love, I am a best-selling author, and *I am prosperous* are all strong affirmations. Can you feel the difference between those statements and *I want to be a best-selling author* or *I will be love, I will prosper*?

Saying these affirmations with gratitude and joy helps you attach positive emotions to the phrases, thus reprogramming your brain even more quickly. You can't be sad if you are repeating how happy and appreciative you are. Try it! An example would be, *I absolutely love and give thanks that I am abundant in all areas of my life.*

As you continue to repeat these statements, new thought patterns will emerge. The longer you repeat your new positive inner chatter, the more these thoughts will become your beliefs, and as you now know, it is your beliefs and feelings that create the world around you. Your inner world is reflected back to you in your outer world. Once this becomes evident to you, believe me, you will do whatever you can to create your dream life in your mind. The results are amazing when we decide to create a more positive inner monologue.

It is important that the affirmations you find or create work for you. Do they make you feel good? Do you want to repeat them? Are they meaningful? Try to feel the essence of the words you repeat. Feel them in your heart and experience the sensations they bring up as you send them into the universe. Know that they can evolve as you do. This is part of the journey. My affirmations have changed over time, and I appreciate that, because they grow as I do.

If you are unsure of what affirmations will work for you, start by saying something that you know makes you feel good. You can say something like, "I am filled with love for my family and friends," or "I am so happy and grateful that my life is filled with love." These two statements are bound to generate feelings of love as you repeat them. One of my favourites, which is simple and very impactful, is, "Life is always working out for me." I love the simplicity in that statement, and when you grasp its truth, it is very liberating.

If you are still having difficulties believing any of the affirmations you find or create, rely on the old adage "Fake it 'til you make it."

It was the use of affirmations that truly began my escape from the childhood memories and beliefs that subconsciously held me back.

Children are sponges

Until the age of about 6, our brains are sponges. We absorb everything with no filters, and it's during these years that many subconscious beliefs are formed. We aren't even aware we are forming them. At this tender age, our young brains cannot properly understand all that is happening around us, and actions can be easily misinterpreted and end up influencing our adult beliefs.

For example, let's say you are 3 years old, and when your dad comes home from work, he normally gives you a hug straight away. However, one day, he has to use the toilet and rushes to the bathroom. He then forgets to give you his typical after-work hug, and your little brain interprets that as *He mustn't love me anymore.* You know he loves you, but your toddler brain can't reason that yet. That one instance can create a lasting impression.

How crazy it that? I often ponder on the process of human development from childhood to adulthood and contemplate how insane it seems that things we don't even understand or have the ability to rationalise as children influence us as adults. The impact of those formative years contributes to who we are and what we think as adults. Imagine a childhood wrought with negativity, neglect, anger, or distrust, and see how easily this can cause issues in your adulthood. It can have a huge effect on people's lives.

It must be so difficult for parents when even the best intentions can be misinterpreted by a young subconscious. No need to fret, though. I am living proof that we have the power to change our negative self-talk and beliefs—and that loving actions, such as meditation and affirmations, can help us every step of the way.

My childhood was bursting with negativity, and I know that had an effect on how I developed into an adult. For many years, I blamed my childhood for all my problems, and it wasn't until I embarked on my journey of love that I reached a stage of actually feeling gratitude and love for everything I experienced growing up. I am a better person because of it, and it led me to where I am today—living a life filled with love.

As I continued my work with affirmations, I deliberately monitored my negative thoughts and replaced them with positive phrases. I wanted to stop the silent self-beratement for good. I remember listening to one of my favourite teachers reiterating what I was hoping for: that affirmations are a great tool for reprogramming our thoughts. I thought, *These are going to become a permanent fixture in my love toolbox. Brilliant!* And with that, another love action was implanted into my life.

I was growing addicted to these good vibrations, and I wanted to see what else I could do to maintain them. Now that it was clear to me how the energy we transmit is based on our thoughts, moods, disposition, and overall state of being—and that it is easily changed simply by adjusting our mental state—I wasn't going to stop. I remember how affirmations began to infiltrate my waking hours and were becoming my new way of thinking. There was a period of about a year after I discovered this powerful tool where I made sure that whenever my brain could be idle during waking hours, I was repeating positive statements, reprogramming my brain.

I was becoming a savvy thinker and pushed myself further, asking, "What else can I do to create an inner world of love?" I was still meditating daily, using tools such as tapping or Emotional Freedom Technique (EFT),[2] repeating my affirmations, and diving into resources that focus on increasing self-love, but I was hungry for more. I took myself a step further and started to pay attention not only to my thoughts but also to my assumptions in situations or scenarios where my knee-jerk reaction was negative. I would ask myself, *What was my initial reaction? What did I assume? How did I feel?*

More often than not, when something came up that wasn't ideal, I would assume the worst-case scenario. My brain would go into a spiral of negative what-ifs, and all that came out of it was unnecessary stress and worry. And it wasn't like this scenario would play itself once in my brain

---

[2] EFT or tapping is a method using acupressure points and certain language to help relieve anxiety and release blocks, negative energy, or limiting beliefs. It is also used to help with things like phobias.

and then float away. No, it would run on a loop, constantly repeating itself until it was all I could think of. It was the next area I needed to focus on improving.

I do think having a cognizance of what *could* go wrong in situations is important, but it's certainly not somewhere we should linger. There's no point in thinking of additional issues or all the things that could go wrong. It does not allow us to approach the situation from a place of solution; rather, it keeps us fixated on problem or worries.

So what I started to do was focus on the best-case scenario instead. I would ask myself, *What could go right? What can I learn from this, gain from this? How will this help me?* These questions often led to solutions or, at the very least, kept my negative thoughts at bay and helped me focus on thoughts that were way more fun.

Practicing the Best-Case-Scenario Game, as I like to call it, and my passion for affirmations continued to rewire my brain. I was opening up to the idea of limitless possibilities and pushing my thoughts in a more loving direction. I began to see that loving yourself is the heart of all love. My loving thoughts and words to myself were making me a better person. My focus was on positivity, and I was charging the energy around me with love and good will. My newly formed relationship with myself made me realise that one cannot love wholly if one does not love oneself.

How can you give love to someone when you can't even give it to yourself? How can you expect someone to love you when you do not love yourself? How do you feel love towards others when you don't feel love towards yourself? When you truly accept your faults, do you accept the faults of others? These questions arose inside me, and the answers helped me approach life differently. My perspective changed. I started to see that self-love is fundamental to humanity's well-being because when you love yourself and fill your life with love, you naturally love others.

But it wasn't until I introduced so much love into my life by putting love into action during my thirty-one-day love challenge that I really saw the full power of love. I now know in my heart that there would be no hate, fear, or anger towards others if everyone truly loved and accepted themselves.

Chapter 3

Throw Your Head Back and Say, "I Quit!"

Sometimes I look at my life and its long string of men and think that these sordid tales of failed *amour* drove me to seek a love that is far beyond what any relationship can give. If I hadn't struggled with romance so much in my life, I don't think I would have ever been tempted to create my own love and eventually learn that romantic love is not the only love I need. Romantic love is merely a miniscule aspect of living a love-filled life, so much so that even if I don't have it, I will still feel loved and loveable, whole, and complete.

I wish I had known that years ago when I believed that finding *the one* was the solution to a loveless life. But I didn't. Instead, lingering in the folds of my mind was the idea that love had to come from others in order to validate my worth. I was blinded by my desire to be married and thinking that if I found Mr. Right, my life would finally be *right*.

Of course, with all the development work I started doing, my self-worth had improved, and the seed of self-love I planted was growing into a beautiful, mighty tree. But I was still a sapling. I yearned for love from someone else and followed the same pattern of believing *any* gesture of affection or interest towards me was worth jumping in head first (often into bed) and assuming *This is it! He's the one.*

Was it because growing up I didn't have the best model of a loving relationship? Was it because my youth was wrought with negativity and unworthiness? Or was it because this was the path I chose when I came into this life? Regardless, for some reason—and I am sure I'm not the only one—I had it in my head that if I gave my body, he would want my heart. I thought the faster I fell into bed, the faster we'd fall in love and live happily ever after. Decades later, I was still behaving this way, even when I knew it wasn't true. There was a part of me living in my comfort zone despite the fact that it actually wasn't comfortable at all.

When the norm isn't right

I was so used to giving myself away physically, despite this newly constructed path guiding me towards self-love, that I continued to throw my clothes to the floor, grasping for the smallest chance at love. One would think that with all of my failed past experiences, I would have stopped this behaviour, but my bad habits were too ingrained. It seemed I was trapped in a perpetual loop of casual relationships, flings, friends with benefits, or hopeless crushes that never went anywhere much beyond sex or a few dead-end dates. That was my norm, with a spattering of narcissists to add some spice.

I was so eager to receive love from *someone* that I allowed anyone into my heart whenever there was even the slightest inclination of feelings towards me. I ran with it, imagining a wonderful future together and ignoring the many signs that things were not healthy or what I really wanted. I developed an underlying fixation that always put me on the lookout for love and created an unhealthy need that I was broadcasting far stronger than any burgeoning confident self-love vibes.

No wonder I was dating duds.

Oftentimes, I would overlook my morals, values, and ideals in trying to obtain the love that I thought had to come from a partner and obviously felt was still lacking. Then, I'd beat myself up for finding the wrong love and question why romance seemed to be outside of my life's vernacular. Then, if it was a particularly bad ending, I would fling myself into despair and doubt, letting thoughts of being unlovable percolate. My dating life was a constant ocean swell of hope and ebb of discouragement.

It was after the millionth (OK, slight exaggeration, but it sure felt like this) in a string of failed dates, and after being fatigued by this series of romantic failures, that I'd finally had enough. I made the decision to no longer let myself be with someone who did not lift me up or want me for anything beyond physical pleasure. I was tired of feeling down and using my body as a dating asset. It was time to change my romantic habits to match my new inner monologue of being light and love.

Armed with this decision and a bubbling desire for self-love, I approached dating with higher standards but somehow was still attracting men who were not emotionally available. They were kind but were only after one thing. They just weren't ready to be anything other than casual with me. I couldn't figure out what I was doing wrong. I was frustrated and felt I could no longer be responsible for making romantic decisions. It seemed I never made the right ones and I didn't want to do it any longer!

And then it happened.

No, a boyfriend didn't fall out of the sky. I gave up. Or, more aptly put, I surrendered to a higher power.

Colinda Latour

Surrendering brings comfort

I was walking my dog, Jeffrey, in the early evening and was distracted with thoughts of *Why me? Why can't I find love?* I was still reeling from the last guy who had entered and left my life so quickly. Part of me wanted to quit completely and become a crazy cat lady. But I knew that wasn't what I truly wanted. Plus, I prefer dogs.

I had reached a point where I felt that I could no longer rely on my judgement when it came to romance, and my heart felt battered. I needed a change but had no idea how or what to do. That was when I threw my head back, looked up at the sky, and said out loud to the universe, "All right, I'm done—done looking for men and done looking for love! I leave this up to you now, Source. I surrender my heart to you and release all expectations of finding *the one*. Finding love is no longer up to me, it is up to you, dear Source. I quit!"

Standing in that energy of surrender and release, I felt a sense of relief as years of sorrow began to waft out of my chest in billows of negativity. After, my heart felt lighter, and I felt a warm energy emanating from my chest. I didn't know it at the time, but I believe my heart chakra[3] was opening and releasing the blocks that had held it stagnant and hurt for so long.

That act of surrender was a big leap of faith for me. I wanted to believe in a higher consciousness—I even labelled it *Source*, as I have mentioned—but I still wasn't a 100 per cent believer. I was just so tired of trying to find romance on my own and was so fed up with never getting it right, I thought to myself, *What do I have to lose?*

Nothing, I decided. So I gave myself permission to have faith and surrendered to the view that something bigger

---

[3] The main chakras are energy centres that run along the spine from the base, the root chakra, to slightly above the head, the crown chakra. The heart chakra is associated with the heart and love. It is green in colour.

would look after me. This was a huge sign, though I did not know it at the time, that love was becoming more prevalent in my life. During the thirty-one days of completing my love challenge, I developed unshakeable faith and came to recognise that when you operate from a place of love, there is no need to fret, because love is your guide and will always lead you in the right direction.

That evening, while walking Jeffrey, I surrendered to that *something bigger*. I surrendered to a higher consciousness, Source, and upped my faith in the unseen. I knew I wouldn't have been guided to surrender if there was nothing to surrender, so I gave up control and let go of any attachment to the outcome. I knew it was time for me to trust that no matter what, I would be all right.

I felt a sense of peace wash over me as Jeffrey tugged on his lead and we continued our walk. Gazing up into the darkening sky, I continued my surrender and whispered, "Source, please tell me how to proceed. I am ready to hear your voice and let go of mine."

Moments later, Jeff stopped to sniff something. When I was jerked to a halt with him, the message came through, loud and clear: *Take a break from dating, Colinda. Come off the dating apps and stop wasting your energy elsewhere. Bring that energy back to yourself and work on healing your wounded heart.*

I smiled as the words floated through my mind. I did not question this, just as I didn't question the message to meditate after I whacked my head on the pole. I felt in my heart this was what I had to do.

When I returned home after our walk, I deleted the dating apps from my phone and made a decision to remain celibate and date-free until I was certain my heart was ready. I didn't put a timescale on it; I didn't need to. I needed time to recuperate and tear down the walls I had successfully constructed around my fragile heart. After all the romantic mishaps I allowed in my life, it was time to direct loving energy to me, not guys on Tinder.

I am very grateful for throwing my head back and giving up my need to control romance that evening. It was exactly what I needed to start my ongoing practice of surrender and pursuit of unwavering faith. It was also exactly what I needed to accept that we don't have to worry about everything. We can leave some things to a greater force.

You may find the act of surrender uncomfortable because you feel you are giving up control. That's fine; it's a normal reaction. Humans are obsessed with maintaining control when in reality, we have no control over what happens. All we have control over is how we act and react, because things can change within a breath.

I know I preach about creating our reality through our thoughts and beliefs, and doing what it takes to create a love-filled life, which all sounds very controlling. This may lead you to wonder how I can say we have no control over our lives when I've been taking steps to do precisely that. Is that not the antithesis of what I've been claiming?

Control or no control

When you honestly consider how many things are out of your control—such as the weather, people, time—can you begin to see how control is out of our hands? Yes, we can influence our lives and do what we can to make them the best lives for us, but we can't say with certainty what will happen tomorrow. We put our thoughts into action and believe from doing so that there will be a specific outcome. But how often do things turn out according to plan?

What we have is the *illusion* of control. We like to think everything in our life is wrapped up with a nice ribbon and everything will occur as we imagined. Then the market crashes and you lose your job, or a global pandemic occurs and life grinds to a halt.

Yes, we are responsible for the lives we create, but really, we don't have control over them. All we can do is control how we behave, because anything outside of that is out of our hands. Surrendering to a greater force helps with this. It takes the pressure off and eliminates unnecessary stress and worry. You can now place your trust in the idea that life is always working out and that surrendering allows limitless possibilities to come into your life.

If you are married to the idea of what you want and how you are going to get it, you are limiting your life's path. You are putting yourself in a box and trying to keep it contained. That usually doesn't go very well, because eventually the pressure of being contained causes everything to blow. When you surrender and let go of the ideas of what *must happen* and how it *must occur*, you create the needed willingness and openness for things to appear.

How do you surrender then?

The first thing to do is take that leap. Jump into the idea that you *can* surrender and that there is a higher consciousness (call it what you will), far greater than us, who always has our backs. If you don't believe in a higher consciousness or a greater force and can't imagine surrendering to some godlike phenomenon, don't worry. The act of surrendering even to the idea that things may not go according to plan allows for possibilities and new things to come into your life. Or how about surrendering to the idea that we live in a benevolent universe and that it's not conspiring against us but rather working with us? Surrendering indicates that we are not tied to a way something *must* happen, but rather we are willing to experience anything that *can* happen.

Once you have decided how you would like to surrender—be it to a higher consciousness or simply to the idea that you'll allow anything to happen—sit back, relax, and listen to the messages and ideas that will come. You will receive these ideas through your intuition, your inner voice. If you need help getting in tune with that inner voice, you can use tools such as meditation.

Or try to remember the last time you received a message from your intuition and think of what was present (or absent) from that scenario. Were you calm, listening to music, drifting off to sleep, in nature, exercising, or zoning out as you drove home? Think of what it was like: Did you hear it? Did you feel it somewhere in your body? Did a visual pop into your brain? Asking yourself these questions will help you become more aware of how your intuition communicates and will increase your trust that you are receiving its messages.

When I threw my head back and looked up at the rosy dusk sky that evening, I didn't know what to expect. But when I felt the blocked energy around my heart being released and heard the message to stop dating, I knew I had stumbled onto something. The feeling and the message were visceral, and that in itself caused me to have greater faith in myself and the act of letting go.

Surrendering is an act of self-love because, as I mentioned, it takes the pressure off. You can trust that it will all work out, even if it's not the way you envisaged or wanted. When I asked for help and then handed it all over to Source, I received the assistance I needed. I acted on that answer and remained single and celibate for over a year (longest duration in my dating history). I stayed true to the message I'd received and dove deeper into my love voyage, focusing on healing my heart and relying on my own validation.

During this time, I discovered *mirror work*, a well-known method for improving self-love made popular by Louise Hay. When I read about it, I remember thinking, *Well, there's no one else who is going to look into my eyes and say they love me right now. I may as well do it myself.*

If you haven't heard of mirror work, all it entails is looking in the mirror, into your own eyes, and saying, "I love you." When I first tried this, it brought up a lot of mixed emotions, as it can with many people. I don't think I fully believed the words. I could say them, but I didn't trust they were true. But I didn't give up. I was persistent, because one, I knew I was close, and two, I wanted it to be true. I had done research on this activity, and the results of increased self-love and joy were too good to miss out on, so I committed to work on it multiple times a day. It took a few weeks of this before the words flowed naturally and with truth. When that happened, I actually let out a cheer, and my heart lit up.

I am loved, I am loveable, yes!

It may seem too simple to believe that saying "I love you" to yourself can really improve your disposition, but hearing yourself say those words and seeing the emotions in your eyes and face can rewire your brain to have more positive pathways. Uttering the words *I love you* as you stare into your eyes sends messages of love to your brain instead of the seemingly infinite self-deprecating chatter that brings you down.

If you want to give it a try right now, go for it! Find a mirror, look into your eyes, and say, "I love you."

If this is difficult for you, just as it was for me, that is OK—it is part of the process. For now, use it as a test to see your level of self-love and acceptance. When you try it, see how you feel. Can you do it? What does it feel like? Do you say it with exuberance or dread, or somewhere in between? Does it make you feel uncomfortable, doubtful, or are you pleasantly surprised how easy it is and how good it makes you feel? Do you have a physical reaction—are you jumping up with joy and waving your hands in the air, shouting it to your reflection and everyone on the block, or are you cringing and pulling away as the words drip out of your mouth reluctantly like thick blackstrap molasses?

Your reaction and desire to do it again is your litmus test for where you are on your self-love path. If any negative or uneasy feeling arises when you try this, do not worry. Many people have difficulty telling themselves this. We are not taught to do this growing up or as adults. If you parade around saying you love yourself, it is often misconstrued as cockiness or selfishness. This is unfortunate, because it is absolutely fine to love yourself. In fact, it is a necessity to healthy living.

Loving yourself increases your confidence and self-respect. It boosts your standards of what is acceptable in any relationship, including your relationship with yourself. When you love yourself, you treat yourself better; you eat better, you exercise, you are kinder to yourself, and you appreciate your value and want to put your best self forward. You are happier with yourself, and this happy, loving energy is the energy that is you and the energy you launch into the world.

If you are not able to comfortably say "I love you" while looking into your eyes, there are other things you can do. You can try to say it without looking into the mirror—or if you are not able to say those words at all, then try saying something like, "I am ready to love myself," or "I know people love me, I can love me too." Say what feels good and makes you at least consider the possibility of self-love.

I promise, it is worth it.

Now I adore looking into my eyes and saying, "I love you." It makes me smile every time, and I get tingles all over my skin. I feel it in my heart, and I know that it is true. Doing mirror work for that year was one of the main things that helped me chip away at the barrier I constructed around my heart, which was preventing even me from getting in.

It helped get me to a state where I finally felt ready to date again. I had an abundance of love for myself that was spilling over and available to share with others. With this love came self-respect, and I knew I would no longer tolerate anyone who did not share the same respect or love for me.

I not only fell in love with me, but I fell in love with the high-vibration state that all this love created. I actively pursued sustaining it by keeping love and other high-frequency feelings—such as gratitude, appreciation, compassion, and empathy—active in my thoughts and activities. I was radiating out into the world what I wanted to receive and finally attracted a partner who was buzzing at that high frequency too.

We met and began to date about fifteen months after my romantic pause. It was a very loving, kind, and spiritual relationship that further enforced, for me, the importance of self-love. We lasted almost three years, teaching each other and helping each other grow as we explored our passions and dreams together. We loved each other as much as we could and taught each other what we needed to learn.

But we were at different stages with our self-love and had to part ways in order to continue. He was just beginning, and I had already trodden the dirt path to get to the pavement with not-so-many potholes. This difference may work for others, but for us, we could not cope as a couple. Being with someone who did not love himself put me in the same place I must have put several blokes, and I finally felt what it was like to be on the receiving end of having to validate someone's worth and lovability. It was exhausting and impossible, but it left me with this teaching: No matter how much someone says you are lovable, you won't believe it until you love yourself.

Chapter 4

Your New Story is Yours to Create

That year of celibacy was a godsend. Taking time for myself granted me the freedom and desire to fall in love with *me* instead of focusing elsewhere. My self-respect grew, and I was driven to uncover the limiting beliefs that I knew played a role in my life. I was becoming aware that my childhood, wrought with difficulties and a lack of unconditional love, grossly influenced my mindset and subconscious beliefs when it came to love, especially when it came to *finding the one.*

I know I have been speaking a lot about romance and dating when at the beginning of this book I spoke about finding divine love, but getting to the bottom of my romantic issues shed a lot of light on moving forward with all love. Besides familial love, romantic love seems to be a hot topic when it comes to our lives. It is part of the societal norm, at least in Canada where I grew up. You fall in love, get married, have kids, and live a life of coupledom. For me, that just wasn't happening.

It took a long time to stop questioning why I wasn't married and whether there was something wrong with me. Finally, I started to be content with my life as it was. In fact, this book is pretty much that journey—the journey of stepping out of the need to find love through a partner, finding that love within, and opening one's heart to divine love, which is everywhere all the time.

So, yes, I speak about stages in my life where I yearned for romance but am fully aware that this is no longer the love I seek. In fact, I do not seek love at all, because I have all the love I need. I was unable to get to this stage without going through the steps that got me here. I hope that the challenges and love actions detailed in Part Two will get you there too, without the anguish and suffering.

The culmination of my love journey came when I realised that love wasn't an emotion we receive but rather a state of being that is easily achieved by simply doing loving things. It is now the state of existence I strive to be in as much as possible. To get there, though, I had lessons to learn and wounds to heal.

Throughout the year I stopped dating, I did a lot of work with my inner child to heal her broken heart and help her feel worthy. I used a lot of guided inner-child healing meditations and even experimented with self-hypnosis. Some believe hypnosis is very difficult to achieve by yourself, and I don't know if I was hypnotised the times I tried it, but what I can say is it helped me, just as the meditations did. Both led to invaluable introspection and deep soul-searching, which ultimately led to freedom and release of two fundamental beliefs that held my heart to ransom.

I discovered stories I had been telling myself since I was a toddler—even since I was in the womb, perhaps—that influenced how I interacted and presented myself to the world. These stories weren't true. They were fabrications I came up with when faced with particular situations, but they had a tight hold on my thoughts. The work I did loosened the grip these stories had on my psyche as I dug up the roots that bound them so tightly to my reality.

I am the youngest of six kids born to a single mother. My father left two months after I was born. My mum managed to keep us together, but she struggled to feed us and keep us warm, clothed, and sheltered. She did it, but it was incredibly arduous and exhausting. We lived in a small northern Canadian town that was isolated—and ferociously freezing and dark for several months of the year. It was not an easy environment in which to raise a family.

It wasn't easy for any of us

When Dad abandoned us, he took all the money and left Mum to fend for herself, with all of us kids under 10 years old. Him leaving was momentous and caused ripples of anguish, grief, bitterness, and anger that spread through each of us as we grew up. It also left us in poverty, and my mum with the very difficult task of raising kids with few resources and little support.

My childhood was tarnished by the filter that Dad leaving ruined us, and my self-imposed blame that he left because of me. I wasn't stupid. Even as a young child, I recognised that the timing of his departure and my birth were too darn close to not be related. The three and a half years between my brother and I, with the rest of the four siblings being eighteen to twenty-four months apart, seemed like a chasm—and obviously, in my mind, a mistake that pushed my father out the door.

With my father leaving and my mother never remarrying, I wasn't exposed to a husband-wife relationship, let alone a healthy one. Most of the stories I heard about Dad growing up were not that nice. He was not your ideal husband and/or father. In fact, he was an alcoholic who would leave for days, sometimes without telling Mum where he was going or when he'd be back. When he left for the last time, he drove to British Columbia and abandoned his truck with his wallet and identification so he couldn't be found. He apparently didn't want anything to do with us—and sadly, when the divorce was finalised, the judge told Mum she was entitled to a pittance for support, but would never see it. He was right.

Dad died about nine years later in a fire in Seattle, Washington, in a bath house in the gay village. The fire was suspected to be arson, but it was never solved, and I never got to know my father. Besides his struggle with alcohol, he also struggled with his sexuality. It must not have been easy for him to be bisexual or gay in the remote northern communities he and my mum lived in during the 1960s and '70s. I am fairly certain his life was as dichotomous as my loving/fearful childhood.

A belief so deep I didn't know it was there

My father's abandonment, combined with the fact that both my brothers departed from my life at an early age—one dying and the other being shipped off to boarding school at the tender age of 12—put me in the mindset that all men leave; that was just the way it was. I didn't even know I held this belief until it found its way up from the basement of my subconscious during my year of celibacy. I remember sitting on my sofa, quietly contemplating the men who passed through my life, when these thoughts popped into my consciousness: *Shit, am I attracting men who never stick around because I believe they will leave? Do I believe they leave because of me?*

My head exploded a little with that epiphany.

It made sense. That belief was burrowed deep into my subconscious, living there, constantly influencing my dating and choice of partners. I held onto it so truthfully that it constantly manifested in my life. Men were forever telling me they weren't ready for a relationship, or they didn't want anything more than casual, or I just wasn't right for them.

There was always a reason to end it. But now, I finally realised I was attracting those men into my life because this is what I believed: men left.

Sitting there shaking my head and stroking my chin in careful consideration, I was aghast at what our young minds can create as truths, and then pleasantly pleased with the power we have as adults to unravel those stories that no longer serve—or, more likely, never served at all. I carried that belief with me until I could carry it no longer, and I gave myself the gift of retelling the story that created it.

I knew it would take work to release a belief I'd had for over forty years, but I was willing. I also knew that if I just tried to forget it, it wouldn't leave. It would linger, and it would sneak its way back into my behaviour. I had to replace it with another story and form a new belief.

When you remove a belief that no longer serves you, it leaves a gaping hole ready to be filled, and I prefer to fill it with something that is good for my soul. This was another of the formative actions that skyrocketed my love journey, reinventing the wheel that was spinning, muddying my thoughts all these years. Now, instead of digging myself deeper, I groped my way out with love, perseverance, and a will to change.

We all have the power to reinvent our wheels, and one of the first steps in doing this is recognising your role in the situation. It was such a relief when I finally unearthed my belief that men leave, and took responsibility for my part in bringing these men into my life instead of placing the blame solely on them. I didn't date men who were unavailable because that's how men are; I dated men who were unavailable because that is what I believed. Every man who had any meaning in my life during those formative years, throughout my childhood and teenage years, left. So that is what I believed men did.

It was Dad who formed this belief especially. I used to fantasise he would come kidnap/rescue me in a helicopter and whisk me away to some wonderful life in a city, but then my child brain remembered he had left right after I was born—and left because of me. This was a ludicrous belief but one that slithered into my reality, further proof that our thoughts and beliefs become our reality.

Once I discovered that belief and pondered the absurdity of it, I recognised it was false. Not all men would leave just because my father and brothers did. That doesn't even make sense. How could I place a rule on an entire group of people based on the behaviour of three men, two of whom had no say in the matter of their absence? This belief had been grating on my soul long enough, and it was time to cast it aside and make room for another.

I researched releasing beliefs and dug for ways to help. I knew I had to work on my inner child and felt the best way forward at the time was with guided meditations. I listened to a few and finally settled on one that felt right. It was geared specifically to working on releasing childhood beliefs, and I could feel the power it had as I reached out to my inner child and comforted her. The meditation guided me through speaking to my inner child and reassuring her she was safe and loved, and that I would always be there for her. She would never be abandoned. I practiced it daily, and after about a week of doing this, something released.

That day, just like the others, I settled into a comfortable posture and put my journal with a pen beside me. I wanted to be able to record anything that came up, as it was recommended for this meditation, and I knew journaling would be helpful for me. I put my headphones in and pressed play. It was beautiful and touching, like my inner child finally believed me when I said we are OK and I will never leave. At the end, I flickered my eyes open to come back into the room. I continued to sit for a few moments reflecting, then picked up my journal and started free-writing the words that floated into my consciousness.

Dad did not leave because of you. Even if he did, you gave him the freedom to live the life that he was meant. You gave him the opportunity to be himself, not some family-bound, pretending-to-be-straight-husband, fitting into the clichéd life of having a wife and kids. You gave him freedom.

Those words flowed from my heart and onto the page. When I read them back, I wept. They held such power and allowed me to acknowledge and accept that Dad's leaving had nothing to do with me. I didn't cause him to leave, and even if I played a part, I gave him a new life. I wrote a final clause before I tore the paper out of my journal and crumpled it. I wrote, *My story has changed. I no longer blame myself for your departure. That was your choice, and I hold no responsibility for it. I have a new story now.*

And with the new story of not being responsible for his departure and granting him freedom, I took the paper to the kitchen and lit it on fire over the sink. I did this because for me, one of the simplest acts of release and renewal is to burn something that represents what you want to let go of. Fire is used in many healing ceremonies and is associated with rebirth. Fire often comes with destruction, but out of it also comes new life. Think of a forest fire that tears through the countryside, only to leave evidence of new growth and rebirth the following year as spring approaches.

That new story came from my willingness to let go and no longer remain a prisoner to my limits. It arrived when I made the decision to take responsibility and do what it took to love myself even more and create my own story that served me, one that a 40-plus-year-old came up with and not a toddler with limited cognition.

That meditation and the act of throwing what represented my old story into the fire resonated with me and flipped a switch in my brain. It changed my victim mentality to one of empowerment. I had told my abandonment story so many times in my head that it became the norm, and my psyche ensured I created it in my own life. After I adopted the new story of dad's departure, life continued to improve, and I now had proof that I could change limiting beliefs into enabling ones.

Can I do it again?

I was so thrilled with the outcome of changing my *men always leave* story that I decided it was time to dig further into my limiting beliefs and dispel another one: the idea that I was unworthy of love. I hadn't even fully grasped that this was an underlying theme in my life despite the fact that after so many break-ups, I wondered, *What is wrong with me? Why doesn't anyone want to love me? Am I unlovable?*

These questions ran on repeat every time rejection slammed the door in my face. However, it hadn't occurred to me that perhaps they stemmed from other beliefs I picked up as a child when my brain was so easily influenced. Perhaps they had nothing to do with my lovability but rather with something I invented. I needed to get to the bottom of why I felt this way.

When my father left, my mother was devastated. Any ideas she had of a life with my father were out the window, and honestly, any other dreams she may have had were most likely wiped away at the same time. Her life went from difficult to fucking hard. She was single-handedly raising six kids in a tiny community with limited options for everything: school, work, housing, and men.

Of course, these circumstances affected our childhood and how Mum raised us. It was a contradiction between love and anger, and I found it very confusing. Though there were a lot of *I love you*s and tonnes of hugs, there was also a lot of screaming and fighting. And the fights were often followed by, "Come here and give me a hug." It was unstable and tense, and I never knew where I stood. I spent my time trying to avoid provocation, but it didn't seem to matter. There was always some reason to get yelled at—I didn't iron the clothes correctly, dust the furniture well enough, or respond quickly enough when called.

I felt like I could never win.

Then there were all the wonderful times—camping, or evenings on the beach where we grew up, morning swims, and late nights staying up watching *Star Trek* (my mum was a Trekkie). She taught us to waltz, and there were feasts on the holidays shared with whoever was alone, family and friends. Adventure and creativity were encouraged, and Mum always knew how to throw the best birthday parties, even when we had very little money. She'd conjure up a scavenger hunt with great treasures at the end.

It was a childhood filled with incongruities and uncertainty, but I know she tried her best. She kept us all together, which was nothing short of a miracle. She also kept a lot of anger and bitterness towards my father, right up to the year before she passed.

After one of my energy healings, I told her that my shaman helped Dad pass into the afterworld. He had been trapped between the living and the dead for almost forty years. When I told Mum this, she confessed that about at the same time he was able to move on, she had a lot of anger resurface and was still very furious with his behaviour.

She and I had a number of conversations about this—she on one end of the phone in the same house he left all those years ago, and me thousands of kilometres away on the south shore of England, the land where she was born. Who could blame her? She was deserted, left with nothing but mouths to feed and bodies to clothe. I would be angry and bitter too.

Unfortunately, this anger had an impact on our upbringing. I remember from a young age hiding in my room trying to remove the arguments and yelling from my reality, but it never worked. These fights, even when I wasn't involved, left me feeling unloved and unworthy, wondering what was wrong with us for Mum to be so angry. Of course, at that age, I didn't realise it wasn't about me. It wasn't about any of us, really—it was about Mum's journey and her pain that she was trying to deal with. My young mind did not have the faculties to discern that though, and I grew up feeling I was never good enough, that I was unworthy of her love.

Fast-forward several years. My sister, Mum, and I are in the kitchen—Mum at the counter smoking and making bread, and my sister and me sitting at the table gazing out the window at the bird feeders. I remember it being a light, fun, casual afternoon. We weren't there for any particular reason, just chatting with Mum, discussing memories and possibilities for the future. I was sixteen, and my sister was in her early twenties, married and about to start a family.

It was during this conversation that Mum decided to tell me she walked the floor for weeks during her pregnancy with me, debating whether she should have an abortion. When she said that, everything dropped. My shoulders slumped, my smile frowned, and my hands fell heavily to the bench beside my legs. My heart crashed.

I had not expected that, and neither had my sister. We both sat there with shocked expressions, thinking, *Bloody hell, why did she tell us that?* When Mum saw the looks on our faces, she quickly tried to save the situation by murmuring something along the lines of, "Well, you're here, aren't you? I obviously decided against it!"

Fair point, but my 16-year-old brain didn't see it that way. Instead, for about thirty years, I held on to the story that Mum didn't want me. Even though she decided against terminating her pregnancy, I was deeply saddened (as a 16-year-old would be) that she even considered it. After she told me this, my mind spun with the thoughts, *Dad didn't want me, and now I learn Mum didn't want me either. I guess I'm not worthy of their love.* My subconscious took a hold of that and piled it on top of the other limiting beliefs, adding more doubts and fears surrounding my lovability.

You will know when it's time to let go

The memory of that talk kept resurfacing throughout the year. I tried to stifle it, but it kept niggling at my heart. I was so used to operating in a comfort zone of unworthiness, I wasn't letting this belief go easily. All the mirror work and inner-child meditations paid off, though, and I finally had enough with doubting my worth and decided to forge forward in determining what was causing it. Next time that memory presented itself, I didn't push it down. Instead, I asked, *What is it telling me?*

Sitting quietly, breathing deeply, I waited for the answer. And it came. It came in a torrent of images of my childhood, ending with the day in the kitchen when I decided Mum had not wanted me. That in itself was liberating, but not quite enough to heal fully. I knew what I needed to do and, armed with the success of retelling my father's abandonment story, I decided to let this story go too. It was time.

For this, I decided to try self-hypnosis. I wanted to find something that could take me back to being in the womb, as I felt that is where the story began. I wanted to work on healing what I may have encountered while Mum had her doubts and deliberations. It took some research and experimenting with different guided hypnoses, but I decided on one by Marissa Peer, a world-renowned speaker and therapist who uses hypnosis as one of her methods. Again,

I used the virtual world of online videos and played a few of her guided hypnoses until I found one that resonated.

If you wish to experiment with self-hypnosis or different forms of meditation, I strongly recommend trying a few until you find something or someone who works for you. These choices are very personal, and it took me some trial and error before I found something that worked for me and I liked.

When I decided it was the right time to try to release that story once and for all, I closed my bedroom door, found a comfortable posture, and sat listening, quietly following the instructions. I relaxed deeper as my breath slowed and grew longer. The spoken words pulled me into the past to my first memories, and I was guided to sit with those for a while before the hypnosis took me even further back.

It guided me to my mother's womb, imagining growing inside her and what it must have felt like: warm, cosy, and wet. It was during this part that my emotional floodgates opened, and I sobbed. I released so much pent-up sadness and blame. I could feel those emotions flushing out of my system and forgiveness dancing in.

I was guided to a state where I could empathise with my mother. I felt the pain she felt when having thoughts of abortion. She did not like those thoughts but also knew what having me would likely mean. She was torn, and I could feel it.

I no longer held the bitterness and anger towards her for telling me that story. I forgave her for having those thoughts, and I forgave myself for feeling unworthy. By the time I was guided back to the room and my physical self, I had so much love in my heart from that beautiful experience, I conjured up a new love-filled story. It came straight from my heart, and when I heard it, I felt the words surround me in a loving embrace.

My inner voice simply stated, *She chose to have me.*

She did not abort me, regardless of the hardships she'd face. Instead, she wanted to have me. She chose me. She decided I was worth whatever problems she would encounter, and that took immense love and courage.

This new story was liberating, and my love for her increased, because now I had empathy and compassion in my heart instead of anger and sadness. It caused another shift in my energy. I was raising my energetic vibration as more love flowed through me, and my imagined fables of being unlovable fluttered away.

Whether I was properly hypnotised or not didn't matter. I was in that deep state of relaxation, and the guidance I received was exactly what I needed. My heart swells when I think of the love and forgiveness that spilled out of me during that guided session.

This brings me to another topic important for living a love-filled life: forgiveness. I cannot stress enough the power of it. I tear up thinking of all the love I gained through forgiving. It can be hard and may not happen immediately. It is an ongoing process, but it is worth every step along the way.

Forgiveness is easier when you have decided to stop letting others negatively impact your life and hold yourself accountable for your state of being. By this time, I knew I was responsible for my emotions, and if part of the deal for cleaning those emotions up was to forgive those who I felt wronged me, then that is what I had to do.

It is not up to others to say *sorry*. That should not even matter to you. It is not about the other person at all. It is about freeing yourself and letting love in instead. Forgiveness does not mean you are OK with what the person did or said; it means you see yourself as worthy enough not to let their actions or words impact you in a negative way. Their wrongdoings are not worth messing up your life. Trust me.

If you are thinking, *This makes sense, but I still get really angry when I think of the person or situation,* then you need to work on yourself a bit more. Ask yourself, *Is it worth me feeling this way? Does it help me to harbour ill feelings, or is it better if I let them go?*

Forgiveness is not a one-time thing. It is an ongoing journey, and part of that journey is forgiving yourself as well. You may not like the way you acted in retaliation or response to a situation or how you still act and feel when confronted with it. It's OK. Trust those feelings and recognise them for the sign they are. Then ask yourself, *Am I ready to release this anger/resentment? Am I ready to free myself from this negativity? Am I ready to forgive?*

You will know when you are ready. One day, you will have had enough, and you'll know it's time to gain your power back. That is how I felt when releasing the story of Mum considering aborting me. I no longer wanted to feel that resentment towards her for thoughts she had well over forty years ago, and that is why forgiveness flooded my consciousness as love poured in. I was ready to free myself from feeling unworthy. I was ready to stop suffering.

It is not our responsibility to change the person who did something to us. We will suffer even more if we try to do that. Our responsibility lies with how we feel and react. This is our power and the power of forgiveness setting us on a journey filled with love.

It was a great relief to let go of those negative stories and replace them with tales that bring a smile to my face. But I know versions of those limiting beliefs will crop up from time to time; that in life is certain. Throughout our lives, we need to relearn lessons, or we may find ourselves reverting to a previous version of ourselves before something inside says, *No, that's the old me.*

If you find yourself in a situation that triggers limiting beliefs you thought you had released, or puts you back in a comfort zone you know isn't right, treat yourself gently and with love. It is understandable for things to resurface, because more often than not, those limiting beliefs have been with you far longer than your new beliefs. It will take time and require repetition of the new story. Be patient and know the hard work is done.

When those heavy burdens left my reality, noticeable moments of bliss began to appear in my existence. Whether I was walking from the tube to work or sitting quietly by the Thames, it did not matter—I would find myself surreptitiously grinning with feelings of lightness and love as I went about my day. I did not realise it at the time, but now I know it was because love was flowing. I was no longer gripping the unloving blame for my father's departure or the stifling sorrow because I thought my mother hadn't wanted me. Instead, I had real, positive stories overtaking my old thoughts. I was living a new life flourishing with love, and I wanted more.

Chapter 5

Becoming Love

It was time to up my love game. I was really proud of how far I had come, but now I wanted more. I wanted to exist in this new and refreshing life of love. I wanted loving healing energy to flow within me and emanate out of me, surrounding my environment so people felt it radiating off me and it made them feel good. I had no idea how to consistently achieve this, but I was determined. I conducted further research into existing in these high-vibration states and discovered the Solfeggio Frequencies and Dr David Hawkins' *Levels of Consciousness*.

The Solfeggio Frequencies are thought to have first been produced as religious music dating back to the tenth century. They are part of a six-tone scale and range from 174 Hz to 963 Hz. Each of these vibrational tones is attributed to various healing capabilities and states of emotional well-being. To put these into a context that may be familiar, the Gregorian chants are in the Solfeggio Frequencies.

The frequency associated with love is 528 Hz and, within this context, is referred to as the *love frequency* or the *miracle frequency* because it is believed to be one of the most powerful frequencies and is considered transformational and healing. Some information I encountered claims that this frequency is linked to DNA repair. To me, this makes sense.

I am sure you have heard that *love heals*, and you can probably attest to it by looking back on your life and remembering the first time one of your parents gave your boo-boo a kiss and made it feel better. Or maybe you can recall the first time a lover held your hand and how wonderful it made you feel.

When I came across Dr Hawkins' *Levels of Consciousness*, this also made sense. It is a scale of states of being with enlightenment at the top and considered ultimate consciousness. Based on its numerical cycle, enlightenment is above 700 and love is ranked at above 500, starting with shame at 20. Dr Hawkins came up with a way to test the light, electromagnetic waves, and sound coming off the heart when someone is thinking and feeling. Based on his studies and data gathered, he created a logarithmic scale to measure the various states, as mentioned above. The positive states are higher up the scale and negative states—such as anger, depression, and fear—are lower. This taught me there is an order to which things can improve and reiterated that you can't go from sad to glad in one shot; it may take some time and work.

The important thing is to be happy with your progress, no matter how small you feel it is. When you look at the numerous diagrams of Dr Hawkins' levels of consciousness, you can gauge where you are and see the next stages of improvement, or decline for that matter, and decide which direction you want to go.

Learning all this was helpful, but I was still struggling with maintaining that loving state throughout the day when I wasn't doing things such as my regular meditation or affirmations. I wanted all the chemicals that are released with feelings of love—dopamine, oxytocin, and serotonin—to flow freely without conditions, and I didn't want to rely on anyone else to achieve that.

It was as if I had reached a love peak and was now plateauing. Even the beautiful mantra *I am love, I am light* wasn't enough anymore. It felt great, but I no longer felt like it was true. I needed something beyond my current love practice to summit that next peak.

From grief comes love

It was during a time of grieving that the solution came to me. In the thick of the first year of the pandemic, one of my sisters passed away. It was during the first lockdown, and I was unable to go home to Canada from England. My family and I grieved continents apart, and I lost all creative ability.

Up to that point, I had struggled to find the right content and tone for this book. I knew I wanted to write about love but was unable to clearly express a meaningful message. I probably drafted ten first chapters, all of which I didn't like. Then, when my sister died, all ideas left me, and I felt withdrawn, lonely, and sad. It was as if my creative energy transmuted into grieving, and I was left to wallow. I could not come up with a single worthy thought that justified putting my pen to paper or my fingers to the keys.

About three weeks after her passing, I woke up and thought, *Enough is enough.* It was time to unblock myself. I was lying in bed comfortably doing my morning routine, and when it came time to set my intention for the day, immediately these words came to me: *Today, you will write. It does not have to be your book; just write anything.*

With those words in mind, I threw back my duvet and flung my feet to the floor. I was determined. I grabbed my notebook, put the coffee on, and got set up to write in my garden. It was a gorgeous sunny day in late September, and I was going to take advantage of it.

I settled into the sun and picked up my pen. I twirled it between my fingers, chewed on its tip, dropped it to the paper, and *hmmmm'd*.

Nothing.

I drained my first cup of coffee and sighed, exasperated. After a second and third cup, deep in frustration and over an hour of getting nowhere, two questions came to me: *What do you want with life, Colinda?* and *What do you want with this book?*

I wrote these questions down in my notebook, and within seconds, my hand started scribbling, and the answers came: *I want this book to bring love, and I want to be love.*

I sat back and smiled. The simplicity of my response was exactly what I needed to spur on further thoughts. I wrote:

> I want to create a lifestyle of love and have love be at the forefront of all my interactions, actions, and thoughts. I want to spread love and project it into the universe. I want to teach people how to do this for themselves. I want my love to inspire others to love and create a world of love ...

My next thought, was *How the heck do I go about this?*

My brain started churning, and ideas glided into my consciousness. Seeing as my current daily rituals were not sustaining the love vibration I wanted and simply speaking the words *I am love* no longer did it either, I thought to myself, *I need to put love into action. I need to* do *love.*

With this fresh idea of *doing* love, more ideas came, and the thought of giving myself a *love challenge* sprouted in my brain. I liked that idea immediately. I love a good challenge, and I could feel the formation of an awesome plan. This was exciting. My pen couldn't keep up as the ideas poured onto the pages of all the "love actions" I could do.

Next came the practicalities—*How long would it be? How many love actions should there be? How many times would I do them? How would I record it? Would I have to document the findings?* These whirling thoughts then led to, *What would the findings even be? What would happen when I introduced so much love into my life by doing loving activities throughout the day? What would be the love side effects, if any?* The questions and ideas kept sprouting as this love challenge came to life. I was giddy with joy, and I hadn't even begun.

After an hour of dreaming up ideas, I decided I would do ten love actions per day for a month, and seeing as October was only days away, thirty-one days was the target. Over the next few days, I frantically prepared for the challenge. I ordered a camera, lighting, and a microphone so I could record daily videos. I found a blank journal and put that aside for daily entries. I prepared a checklist so I could track the number of times I did each action and prepared myself for a love bombardment.

I had no expectations but hoped that, somehow, I could measure any changes caused by introducing buckets of love into my life. If you asked me then what I thought might come from this, I wouldn't have been able to speculate beyond *I'll feel better*. However, only days into it, I knew that the results from *doing* love would change my life. I am blown away by all the amazing things that occurred during and after those thirty-one days. Even on day one, it was evident that this challenge would have a huge impact. I remember asking myself what I enjoyed the most on the first day, and this is what I wrote in my journal:

> All of it! The washing my hands with love, feeling the warm water lather up my favourite Turkish bath soap, the love meditations and snuggling with Jeffrey my dog for a glorious

fifteen minutes. The giving praise to my co-worker and sending loving messages to friends.

I want to make people's lives better. I want everyone to feel love and be love, and I hope this challenge will help with that.

Even after more than a year since completing the challenge, I still resonate at a higher frequency, operate from a place of love more consistently, and feel the love all around me. I love and know myself well beyond what I thought was possible and learnt so much about love and its powers during those thirty-one days. I cannot express my gratitude enough for all the shit that transpired in my life to get me to the point of wanting such a challenge.

When deciding upon the love actions, I knew they had to be easy, not contingent on someone else's love, and not too time-consuming. I wanted measurable activities that could be done throughout the day with little disturbance to my normal work/life activities. They also had to be a good mix of self-love actions, love actions towards others, and love actions that purely focused on generating loving feelings.

Love actions change your world!

I came up with what I believe is the perfect set of love actions that can be easily spread throughout the day, even when completing some of them multiple times each twenty-four hours. Some of them I already did daily, some you have read about in previous chapters, and others were brand new. The actions are:

- Hug Yourself
- Meditate
- Heart Breath
- Love in the Mundane

Living in Love

- Luscious Luxury Love Moments
- Affirmations and Mirror Work
- Letting Go/Surrender
- Sending Love
- Things I Love
- Loving Kindness Meditation

You can find descriptions of each of these in Part Two, Chapter 8.

Throughout the challenge, which I call the Full-On Love Challenge, I tracked the number of times I did each love action to make sure I didn't miss any and to ensure I at least did the minimum requirement I set. As the month progressed, I increased the number of times I did some of the actions because I couldn't help but want to fill as many hours of the day as possible with love. The more love I generated, the more I wanted, and the more I wanted, the more I generated. I had created a perpetual love cycle, and it was heavenly.

I was able to reach that next love summit I yearned for with this challenge and experienced results I hadn't fathomed. I noticed differences within the first few days but had no idea of the profound effects, gifts, and teachings that would prevail during the month and endlessly after. Not only did I achieve exactly what I wanted to by the time the challenge ended (act, react, and communicate from a place of love as much as possible) but I *became* love. My thoughts and actions were transformed by this new love-filled state of being, and my conscious and subconscious minds were greatly influenced by the new energy that I generated. Putting love into action put me in a high vibration state and created a reality I dubbed *living in love*.[4]

---

[4] The results and outcomes I describe in this book are based on completing the Full-On Love Challenge in its entirety in thirty-one days. Some days I did more than the minimum requirement.

In my new reality, I experienced sustained periods of bliss, profound connections to Source, a sense of wholeness, and being at one with everything. I felt lighter and more aware of my energy body and the energy around me that I was emanating into the world. Any doubt I had of a higher consciousness and being one with the universe vanished as my faith skyrocketed. As love seeped into the cells of my body, I felt secure and worry-free.

As each side effect of love, as I sometimes refer to them, unfolded, I noticed how they all fed into each other and created an even more love-filled environment and state of being. For example, doing ten acts of love each day brought me great bliss because when you are engulfed in love, it is easy to be blissful. Having sustained periods of bliss helped me feel whole and complete, which made me feel even more love: love for me and love for the world I am part of. This sense of wholeness went beyond my physical body, and I felt connected to everything through the loving energy that is the soul of our existence.

Energy and connection

One of the most magical moments on this journey happened on day sixteen, right around the halfway mark, when I was walking my dog. Jeff and I regularly walk in this large cemetery that has plenty of green space and is always bustling with squirrels, birds, dog walkers, and visitors. It was on such a walk that I felt a true, unmistakeable connection to Source. On the days leading up to it, I could feel energy buzzing around me while Jeff and I floundered in the fallen leaves. I chalked it up to the animals scurrying about preparing for winter, but there was more to it.

When I walked through the cemetery gate and onto the grass, I could feel the difference. It was like nature

Living in Love

provided a portal for me to get closer to Source. Everything glistened and shone multitudes brighter, clearer, and sharper than previously, with the depths of green in a single leaf mesmerising me. The world was moving under my feet, and the air carried sparks of energy that gleamed as I breathed in the fresh air. I felt a deep love for everything, and I sensed life everywhere.

My eyes opened wider, and I took deeper breaths, wanting to capture and hold on to this experience. As I stroked the bark of one of the trees, my hand melted into its roughness, and we became one. It was in this moment that I knew without a doubt that I was part of the bigger picture. I was a part of everything. There was no separation. All the love in my life transported me to another dimension, it seemed, one much more vibrant and tangibly connected.

I had felt connection to Source before, especially in nature, but this was stronger, more encompassing. It wasn't a feeling; it was reality. The creator, Source, was there beside me, with me, *was* me—Source, or Divine Love, was all-encompassing, and I was at the heart of it. It lasted the entire walk, and I didn't want it to end.

I felt complete as I walked amongst the animals and trees and felt the air travel through my body and out into the universe as I breathed. The only other times I felt such oneness were a few occasions swimming when I'd become so entranced with being present, I could not tell when my body ended and the water began. Day sixteen flung me past the fleeting suspicion we are all one and landed me in absolute comprehension that we are one with everything, including the divine.

It became evident after this magnificent day that I could turn that connection to Source on again simply by thinking of it. All I have to do is take a few deep breaths, calm my mind, and feel the love flow through me. I mentally say, *I am love, light, and space,* and envision my physical body fading.

I picture existing as energy and not matter. I let the lines of my body blur from my senses. I project myself into the space that surrounds me and focus on love. It is like Roger Bannister's four-minute mile that no one thought could be done until he did it. Then, within just over a year, four other people broke the same record. Once the belief is present, it can be accomplished again and again. For me, it was as if love unlocked a padlock and opened the gates to Source energy and bliss.

As the challenge progressed and I continued to grow as a loving being, I could easily tune in to energy fields. I became intensely aware of my own energy and any changes to it, as well as the energy surrounding people and objects. It makes sense to me now, but it was not something I predicted. When we are happy and love-filled, we feel lighter, more energy-based. Whereas when we are sad or upset, we feel heavier and are more mass than energy.

Have you noticed this? Is it not evident in our own physicality? When you are blissful and feeling love, you skip along as if you are as light as a helium balloon. But when you are sad, you drag your feet and slump your shoulders. You feel heavier, dragged down. Living in a state of love raises our vibration and gives us that flight-y, air-y feeling, and we become more astute to the energy we are broadcasting.

Faith, bliss, and manifesting

These experiences expanded my personal faith and my faith in a benevolent consciousness. I felt as if I could accomplish anything and had the support of the universe. Love was generating a life I wanted, and serendipitous events became a regular part of my day. I was filled with so much love that I was whole; there was nothing missing from my life.

I didn't even have to focus on things I wanted. All I had to do was *do love* and reap the rewards. From this state of love, I manifested things like crazy! I mean, we are always manifesting. That is the nature of life. But these were people and things I may have had a fleeting thought about, and *voila!* They were at my doorstep. This new, seemingly simple manifesting prowess increased my faith and bliss even more.

At first, I was surprised at this. It did not even occur to me that introducing love into my life could conjure things up. So it took a while for me to figure out *how* love was the key to effortless, fast-track creation.

Months after I completed the challenge, I finally put my finger on it. There are two reasons I discovered, based on my experience. One is that when we exist in a state of love, we are not blocking anything. We are open and allowing, because with this loving feeling comes trust and wholeness. When we feel whole, we do not feel lack. We know there is nothing missing, and when nothing is missing, that is when more shows up. Lack attracts lack, but love attracts whatever you want, because in your emotional state and energetic vibration, you already have it. You need nothing else when you live in love, and the universe responds by making your life even better than it was.

Which brings me to the second reason: It's all about how we feel. If we are blissful, content, and feeling great about life, guess what? That is what we attract—more things to make us feel happy, contented, and wonderful.

If you ask yourself why you want something you don't have, the real answer, when you drill it down, is that it will make you feel good or better than you already do. And if you are already feeling awesome, more awesomeness appears. Our emotions are an integral force when it comes to attracting and manifesting, so when I was living in a state of love from all the love actions I was completing, life just gave me more reasons to feel love.

We are responsible for the life we create and what we bring into it, and when we realise we can manipulate what we manifest into our existence, it's exciting. And when we start doing it, that is life-changing. Suddenly, our eyes are opened to the power we possess.

Those who are familiar with manifesting and have tried different methods for bringing something or someone into their life may not believe that over the course of the thirty-one days of my love challenge, I didn't do anything consciously to manifest things or people. I didn't visualise, create a vision board, or write things down repeatedly. In fact, I barely put any thought into what I wanted. One, because there really wasn't anything I wanted; I was filled with love and peace, so what else did I need? And two, I didn't have to; love was doing the work for me.

Money is often a hot manifesting topic, for myself as well. In fact, I spent a lot of time changing my thoughts and beliefs about money, going from not enough to feelings of abundance. But I still had limiting beliefs about it.

This changed when love became my main focus. Money started flying into my life! First, there was an unexpected decrease in my rent. Then came the unexpected announcement that we would receive a bonus at work. A few days after that, work also announced we were getting a raise. It was mad how money just showed up, and it didn't stop. Less than a year later, I was offered a job that paid twice what I had been earning.

The same thing happened with people. Throughout the month, I would think of someone, and moments later, I would hear from them. It got to the point where I expected my phone to buzz whenever I thought of someone.

Then there was the manifestation of my lover who I was seeing at the time. On a number of occasions, I'd be thinking of him, and he would show up within the hour unannounced. Or he'd pop into my head, and next thing, he's messaging to ask if he can see me that day. I was a manifesting machine, and it was all because of love.

Doing loving things so intensely for that month filled my life with bliss, contentment, peace, and wholeness. I knew in my heart and head that I lacked nothing, that anything was available to me, and frankly, I had all I needed and then some. That was the message being broadcast into the universe by my vibrating being, and that was what I got back—more things to make me feel loved, whole, and at peace.

Intuition and trust

Opening my heart to love opened my heart to me and the greater consciousness that exists within. We are blessed to have an inner being who always operates from a place of love and leads us down the path of least resistance and joy. Unfortunately, we often don't hear or trust it. I pushed my inner voice aside a number of times, but as I introduced more love actions into my life, especially meditation and surrendering, my intuition blossomed into a voice I could acknowledge and trust. Now I hear and feel it loud and clear, and when it is speaking, I follow what it suggests. Your guide will never shout or yell. It only speaks with love.

This increased capability to recognise my inner guide led to better decisions. Better decisions led to more love. More love led to less judgement and greater acceptance of myself and others. Greater acceptance led to more empathy and compassion and a new approach to life, one with an open, accepting heart. An open and accepting heart increased my trust that my life was exactly where it was meant to be.

I stopped worrying about the future because love taught me to be present. It is hard not to live *right now* when love is your dominant state, because you have nowhere else to be. You are neither sad about the past nor anxious about the future, and you know life is always working out. *Doing love* kept me in the here and now, and if I did think about what was to come, it was from a place of love, and the outcome never mattered. All that mattered was I knew it would work out, because I had love on my side.

There is no denying that with greater love, you feel fantastic. Even more than a year after completing my thirty-one-day love challenge, I am still less stressed, more relaxed, and in happier moods more of the time. My elevated moods are consistently lengthy, with only minor hiccups that rarely bring me down for long. When they do, I reach into my love toolbox and start doing more loving things.

Love has become my point of reference for solving problems and managing life. My worries are no longer my own; I have love to help. My sadness is not suffered silently; I have love to dry my tears. My happiness is not shouted solo; love hands me the megaphone to make my voice louder. My faith is not left pondering; love serves it to me on a silver platter.

All the work I did leading up to this challenge got me to the place I needed to be in order to 1) come up with the challenge and 2) be ready for it. I had finally arrived at a place where I knew love was more than romance, friendship, family, and caring for places, animals, and things. Love was a state of being I could achieve by myself. The challenge lifted me to such high levels of understanding and living that it was the greatest contributor to transforming my life. I went from fear-based living to being love. I went from feeling unworthy of love to feeling worthy to spread love wherever I went. Having so much love in my system brings pure ecstasy. It is long-lasting and forever-returning, even if I doubt its presence.

Love is my guide, my friend, my family, myself. It is with me every step of the way and will be forever.

Chapter 6

The Divine Omnipresence that is Love

Beyond the bliss, faith, wholeness, and connection I described in Chapter 5, there were two other outcomes from my challenge that have significantly impacted my life. The first, which I have touched on before, is that love is divine. I want to expand on this notion and share with you some experiences I had during the challenge that cemented love's divinity, in the sense of how it can improve all aspects of our life and how it is always available. It is the notion that love is omnipresent and is our natural state of being.

The challenge did exactly what I hoped for. Love became me, and I became love. There was so little effort to get to this point. It astounded me how simple love truly was, and I wondered why it had been lacking for so long in my life. All I had to do was love things and think loving thoughts, and love seemed to grow exponentially around me.

The second greatest gift I received during this month was the proof that spreading love and sending it to others, mentally or physically, not only benefits them but you as well. There is no other thing, in my mind, that can get you out of a slump faster than doing loving things or thinking loving thoughts for others. Giving love is one of the simplest and most powerful tools for improving your life.

Love at the workplace

One of the biggest challenges for me as an adult, especially in the last ten or so years, is appreciating my day job and bringing love into the workplace. This is because in my heart, I know I am a writer and struggle with the fact that I am not doing it full time (yet). Fortunately, I love my profession and am good at it, so that is a bonus. But I still need to let go of the resentment that surfaces from time to time.

On day thirteen, that was what I released. I released feeling distraught that my sole career was not that of an author, and I embraced all the wonderful things I loved about my profession and how much fun I'd had over the years learning and progressing in it. I let go of yearning to be only a writer and showered the practical *I need a job* side of me with love. This was a great help in finally arriving at the day when love became my go-to response at work.

Love at the workplace was always in the back of my mind when I created and implemented this challenge, because I wanted to ensure that love was present in all aspects of my life, including work. It can be one of the biggest stressors in life, and I didn't want that in mine. So I was incredibly grateful when love seeped into all hours of my day.

Even when you love your job, it can still cause stress and anguish. Imagine what it's like for those who really dislike or hate their job? It must be awful. If you are one of those people, I promise, love can help. Performing loving actions will recalibrate your emotional set-point and have you approach everything you do, including your nine-to-five, with a loving attitude. Love may not make you *love* your job, but you will certainly feel less stressed about it, because as you change your approach to thinking, communicating, and acting to be more love-filled, you will change your outcomes.

It was about a week after I let go of my career resentment that a situation presented itself at work where I could have easily acted from a place of stress and fear. Instead, I acted from a place of love, and the beauty of it is that what I did here can easily be applied to any area of your life. If you follow this same principle when dealing with your family, romance, friends, and even yourself, you will notice a change in response or reaction from the people you are dealing with.

On this day, I was given a task that was beyond my capability to complete in the time that I was given, and I knew I had to tell my manager that I would require extra time and assistance from others. This piece of work had been rolling around for months and was an ongoing stressor, and I knew things could blow up about it. When my manager video-called me to discuss it, this thought flickered into my consciousness as I picked up my headset: *Put a smile on your face and act with love.*

That instruction came from my heart, and at the exact time I needed it, because hearing it then changed my approach. Instead of being upset, which I was before picking up the call, I asked myself, *How can I make this the best for everyone? How can I solve this problem without disturbing or upsetting others?* That change in mentality ended in a great discussion that moved the project forward in a way that satisfied everyone.

Love bolstered the reception to my inner being's guidance to take the call with love and opened my heart to be kinder. It was an eye-opener for me, and one that I look back on frequently when I need a reminder to approach all things with love, even when I don't like the situation. Now, as a constant reminder, I have a sign above my computer monitor that says, "Love at work always," and what a difference that mentality has made.

This is a wonderful example of the power of love and how it can transcend any problem or issue. You just need to apply it to those situations, or as was the case on that day, have your life filled with so much love, it oozes out at any opportunity. It is an example of when love is divine—when you hear your intuition, your higher-self—and it is guiding you to be love.

Love heals and is always with us

It may sound like I mostly floated along on a fluffy cloud of love for that month and thereafter, but that wasn't the case. Even when you are inundated with love, there can be down days. Experiencing this helped me grow and understand love even more. I learnt that even when everything hurt, love will still guide you to a better place, even if you don't think so.

On day nineteen of the challenge, I was feeling low. It was six weeks since my sister had passed, and I had recently learnt that my mother had lung cancer, which was unexpected (months later, we learnt she was misdiagnosed). I had a moment of anxiety where I felt overwhelmed with everything and my body ached. I needed to speak to someone for support, but I wasn't sure who.

I asked my inner being for direction, and right away, my friend's name came to mind. I called her moments later, and it was perfect. She provided a different perspective that helped me through this difficult period, with her words prompting me to research love deeper.

When I told her how I was aching and distraught, she said I was feeling sad and hurt because I loved so much. I hurt because I loved my sister, and she was gone. I hurt because I loved my mum and was sad that I could not be there for her. It was a beautiful perspective, exactly what I needed to hear, and I appreciated it wholly. But it made me question: Does love hurt?

My immediate answer was *no*, but I could see what my friend was saying and pondered the idea. I was feeling low because I loved my sister, and she could no longer return that love. I hurt because I loved my mum and couldn't do much beyond call her. Both were painful experiences involving love.

Then my brain kicked in and said, *Wait, that's not love hurting. That's the absence of love and inability to help someone I love. Love can't hurt; love brings comfort.*

With that in mind, I began to scour the internet to see what other people thought about it. I found several studies, some dating back to the 1970s, which all concluded that emotional and physical pain are registered almost the same way in our brain, thus feeling the same. Many of the studies I found had performed similar experiments to come to this conclusion. The testers excluded people from social activities and measured how they felt in that situation compared to a physical sensation of pain. The results indicated the same brain patterns occurred for both the physical and emotional stress, providing evidence that feelings of loss or lack of love could feel the same as a physical hurt.

I was fascinated by this, and it proved to me that *love* did not hurt. Rather, the hurt comes from the feelings that arise when love is removed or altered in some way that prevents it from continuing. *That's* what hurts.

While reading about this, I started to feel great waves of warmth and comfort. I was still not blissful or smiling ear to ear, but I felt great love. And that is when I felt the truth: love is omnipresent. It is always with us, regardless of how we feel. We just need to let it shine through all the hues of darkness or layers of sadness that exist, and it will prevail. We do not have to be in a blissful state to feel love;

it permeates any emotion. It never hurts, but it *may* let you hurt so you can feel it again. It never leaves, but it *may* not be glaringly visible at all times. But we are never alone; love is always present.

After sitting with this for a few moments, letting the love seep into my being, I decided to investigate some more. Now, I wanted to learn of love's healing power. If we can feel badly when it is removed, can we feel better when it is introduced? *Of course*, I thought. *But let's see what others think.*

That was when I found information about an intriguing experiment conducted in 2009. A woman named Sarah Master, who worked at the University of California, Los Angeles, conducted a series of experiments measuring how people feel when exposed to love after being subjected to pain. The test subjects were a group of women who had been in relationships for at least six months.

In the experiment, the women were exposed to heat stimulations. First, the researchers performed tests to determine the women's pain threshold, then the women were subjected to heat either at their threshold level or a degree hotter. The women were then asked to perform a series of tasks to determine if any of the tasks mitigated the pain.

The first series of exercises involved direct contact—first holding their partner's hand when subjected to the heat, then holding a stranger's hand, then holding an object. The second part of the experiment tested indirect contact and had the women look at pictures of their partner, a stranger, or an object when subjected to the heat. The findings noted that contact involving the partner, whether it was direct or visual, resulted in lower pain ratings compared to the other tasks. In fact, looking at the partner's photo led to slightly lower pain ratings than holding their hand.[5]

---

[5] Jaffe, Eric, "Why Love Literally Hurts," *Association for Psychological Science*, 2013 https://www.psychologicalscience.org/observer/why-love-literally-hurts, accessed 10 March 2021.

Isn't that amazing? Does it make your imagination run wild and think how this could impact the world? Our sick, our suffering, our sad? We don't even need direct loving contact to benefit from love's power. Think of the implications this could have if people started to direct love to others, whether present or not. It is truly awesome and inspiring.

When I started this challenge, I was still sad over the passing of my sister. I could not go home because of the global pandemic, and I was in mourning. I found myself crying repeatedly on some days and overwhelmed with sadness because I was so far away and physically disconnected from my family. Those moments lessened greatly as my focus turned from grief to love. It was not the easiest time, but it was probably the best time to introduce boundless love into my life.

Learning what I did from that study gave me proof that love *does* heal. It has the power to help us with any pain, emotional or physical; we just need to allow it or *do* it so we exist in a loving state. That is why doing loving actions consciously throughout the day will improve your life, no matter how good it already is. Though you may not be skipping with joy all the time, love is present and helping you navigate life in a manner that is beneficial to all. As it fills your life, it will radiate to all those around you, and the benefits of being more loving become evident. I promise.

Love begets more love and has the power to lift every soul it touches. When more people realise how easy it is to achieve a state of love simply by putting love into action, it will be a game-changer.

Spread love, it's easy

In line with learning how it can hurt when love is removed and how easy it is to heal with even the idea of love, one of the best things that came out of this challenge was my unrelenting desire and practice of spreading love. Love is addictive and contagious—two things you don't usually think of positively, but in this case, they are stellar! It is the best addiction you can have and one that should be constantly fed so it can grow even more.

The more you love, the more love you feel, and the more you will want, which causes you to add even more loving activities and thoughts into your life. This love then oozes into all facets of your life, further impacting those you interact with and benefiting your own mental state of being.

Here, I want to tell some stories about how I spread love during the challenge (and still do) and the impact these activities had on me. Now I know my purpose in life is to spread as much love as possible and demonstrate how easy it is to transform one's life, and eventually the world, simply by doing loving things. I believe if more people did this, we could collectively influence our surroundings, and this simple idea could have global ramifications. It is up to us to harness the power of love and unleash it onto the world.

As the challenge progressed, so did I. I was an open vessel, and each day, I felt love for me and others grow. I operated more consistently from a state of love, changing my perspective on how to interpret and manage what was happening around me. The lenses I now gazed through had the *approach this situation with love* filter, and I became more caring, thoughtful, and compassionate. Like I said, it was addictive; the urge to do even more love actions transpired, so I increased the repetitions and changed or added new activities.

One change I made was with the Hug Yourself love action. This is primarily a self-love action, but I started using it to share my love with others as well. Seeing as I have moved a lot in my adult life, I have friends all over the world and sometimes I want to give them a hug, but we are physically separated. So what do I do to help with that? I hug myself and think of them.

This started with hugging my mum remotely after she was misdiagnosed and I wanted to support her and be there for her. I started hugging myself several times a day and sent that tender love in her direction. I had a picture from years ago of me and my mum hugging, and it helped me to really feel her presence and the love between us as I wrapped my arms around myself and imagined she was there.

When I amazed myself with how good that felt, I tried it with one of my best friends who lives thousands of kilometres away. She and I are big huggers and will always greet each other with a bear hug when we see each other, but the opportunity to do this in person hadn't appeared in years. So I took it upon myself to hug her mentally. Then I decided, *I'm going to let her know when I do it* and started sending a quick text message saying, "I just hugged you." This started a fun exchange of love we have continued to this day.

This is one very easy and meaningful way to spread love and make yourself feel fantastic at the same time. Remember the experiment where women felt better just looking at a picture of someone they loved? Well, this runs on the same principle. You don't have to physically be there to feel the benefits of love.

Another example of impacting others as well as myself through spreading love presented itself to me during the first lockdown for COVID. Normally, I love grocery shopping. However, during COVID, as I was roaming the aisles, I found I had anger towards those not wearing masks or shoving past me too closely. It became an activity I abhorred instead of adored.

One day, I decided that one of my Sending Love actions would be to send love to everyone in the grocery store when I was there. Before I entered, I took a deep breath and thought only loving and accepting thoughts, as opposed to my fear-based judgement and distrust. I said to myself that I have no idea why people aren't wearing masks; in fact, it is not my business. What I need to do is be more loving to everyone and put that energy out there.

What a difference that loving mindset made! I did this early in the challenge, day five, and it made such an incredible difference in not only how I felt about grocery shopping but how my shopping trips went that I did it every time. I noticed a significant difference in how people behaved around me. People were more polite and considerate, and I could even sense some smiles under all the masks that were worn. I was spreading love, and I was receiving love in return.

As you can see, love is truly a glorious phenomenon that is simple to create and disseminate. Even if you only do a portion of the love actions I mentioned in Chapter 5 and detail in Chapter 8, you will notice significant positive results. It will get to the point where all you want is to exist in a loving state, and you'll find yourself thinking about different ways to do that.

Love from frustration

One of my favourite additional love actions started on day nine when I decided to create love from frustration. For example, I love my dog deeply. He has been a close companion for ten years now, and anyone who has a pet can understand the levels of love we have for them. However, Jeffrey can annoy the crap out of me on our walks when he stops every few seconds to sniff, pee, and sniff some more. What could take ten minutes to walk takes thirty. So on one of our walks, I decided to change my perspective of his behaviour and instead of feeling annoyed every time he stopped, I turned it into love. From then onwards, when he stopped, so

Living in Love

did I. I stopped, took a deep breath into my heart, and sent love to someone.

Throughout those thirty-one days, sometimes I found myself contemplating the benefits of sending love mentally. I know now it has an impact, but I didn't always trust that to be true. I knew that when I sent love through a message, in person, or on a video or phone call, I always received love in return. After I sent my message, I'd receive a text or voice message back proclaiming their love and gratitude for the loving message I sent. It was great, and I felt wonderful for all individuals involved. But did mentally sending love messages have the same impact? The energy and love surrounding the messages were the same—same intent and same feelings—but was that enough to reach the person or people?

I know our emotions and thoughts carry energy. This energy can affect the environment around us and travels as we do. I also know that according to quantum physics and the phenomenon of entanglement, there can be connection at the particle level regardless of how far apart items may be. With those ideas and the changes that were occurring in my life because of love, I concluded that *Yes, absolutely*, even if people cannot physically perceive the love I send, it is reaching them and impacting their energy field.

You can experiment with this. Smile and say, "What a great day!" Now frown and say, "What a sad day." Can you feel the difference in energy? Or how many times have you walked into a room and felt the energy, whether it's happy, sad, angry, or joyous—you can feel it. We are energetic beings and can feel the energy around us, so if you are bombarded with loving energy, guess what? You will feel it. Love can be felt across the room, the city, or around the globe. But do not forget: so can hate and anger. It's up to us to spread love instead.

Confident in this new faith, I began to expand my messages of love and send love to groups of people around the world who were suffering, starting with all the patients in the hospitals near me. This felt amazing. I could feel the love gather around me and travel to the people in my thoughts, and my imagination went crazy as I started to wonder what would happen if love was sent like this on a grand scale. Imagine if fifty more people were doing the same thing right now. Or hundreds, thousands of people did this, and they all deliberately acted from a place of love throughout their day. We would live in a different world.

There are already studies that clearly demonstrate the power of prayer and positive thinking when done as a group, so imagine a world where sending love to everyone was common practice or done regularly by large masses of people. What if sending love became as normal as brushing your teeth?

I loved this action so much, I started to do it with animals and places that I thought needed love. On every walk with Jeffrey and at every stop to sniff the thousands of scents his little nose inhaled, love went out to someone—some place, group, or creature. Our walks of frustration turned into strolls of joy.

If you want to try this exercise, I suggest you pick something that annoys or frustrates you (not too much at first) and turn it into love. For example, if you drive and traffic is slow, instead of feeling annoyed, send love to yourself and all those around you. Or if you get frustrated when your kids leave a mess, send love to the children who don't have a mess to leave. Take any opportunity you can to change negativity into love.

I took this even further on day twenty-seven when I was out with Jeffrey and ended up having nothing short of a miraculous experience. We were walking around the neighbourhood early in the evening when people were settling in for dinner and relaxing after a day's work. On this walk, I decided that every time he stopped, I would direct a loving light from my heart into the house we stopped in front of. I imagined a golden light coming out of my heart and into the home, envisaging joy and love permeating the environment and the occupants inside.

It happened a lot because, as you know, Jeffrey likes to sniff everything, and after the tenth home or so, as I imagined a radiant love beam flow from my heart, the words *It is God's light* came to me. This surprised me because even though I believe in a higher consciousness, at the time, I didn't use the *G* word, instead referring to *Source*. But I took it for what it was worth and felt inspired to continue imagining that the light came from our creator.

Once I received that message, I noticed a change. When I focused on the light coming from my heart and moving into the house, I got a tingly sensation in the back and front of my head and heart. I felt the light shooting out of my chest and back in a column of golden energy that I know came straight from a greater consciousness, through me and into the house in front of me.

It was phenomenal, and what I loved even more is that this feeling came to me so easily on this day. I took full advantage of it and imagined that light providing wellness and blessings to the household. I didn't limit myself to sending love; I wished all the good I could. I was sure it had an impact, especially after learning what I had through my research on how love heals. I had never experienced anything like it and know it happened because my heart was overflowing with love, and I set the intention to send love to the individuals and families within their homes.

Now I experience this whenever I do it. If I set the intention to send love and well-being and focus that love coming from Source, I feel those tingles and God's love radiating out of me. I am a conduit to spread divine love, and there is nothing special about me. All I do is love, and you can do it too.

During that life-changing month, dreams of a world where love was more prevalent continued to percolate. I started fantasising that if everyone created more love in their lives, compassion would become the place humanity operated from. I envisioned our world was run only with kindness and love. I daydreamed of a reality where hate and anger were things of the past and a drive to serve for the betterment of all creatures and Mother Earth was what made the world go round. This became my life's goal and one I now frequently daydream about, plotting its way into existence one love action at a time.

I have faith that not only will love grow but also the desire to spread love, because I am definitely not the only one who feels its importance and power. I believe humanity is on the cusp of a positive transformation, and we have the power of infinite love at our fingertips. When we tap into that endless stream of love simply by *doing* love, we become love-filled beings, just like I have. And love-filled beings, as I discovered, just want to create and spread more love. We become perfect love perpetuators, and who wouldn't want to be that?

On top of knowing the astounding, achievable results from living in love (sustained bliss, greater connection to Source, faith in life and yourself, deep awareness of your energy-body and the energy around you, spontaneous manifestations, and the most beautiful feelings of wholeness and oneness with all of existence), you now have powerful proof that the propagation of love naturally occurs when you do more loving things and think more loving thoughts. The simplicity surprises and invigorates me. I can assure you that if you even picked only two of the love actions from the Love Action Matrix and started doing them daily, you would experience a positive change in your life.

My original intention with the challenge was to see if I could operate consistently from a place of love and raise my natural vibrational setting. I was not thinking on a global scale. However, by the end of the first week, I sensed incredible possibilities that were available by simply introducing a steady cascade of love into my life. About halfway through, I started calling myself a global love generator, because I knew the impact all the love actions I was doing could have on the world if even hundreds of people did them. I regularly engage with a beautiful vision of smiles spreading across faces around the globe as more and more people become love.

We create a world without suffering, a world without hate and discrimination, a world where we treat everyone equally, including all creatures. We respect Mother Earth and all of existence because humanity now operates from love. Everyone has taken the time to work on themselves, to heal their woes, and to partake in the journey of self-love because we know now that loving yourself is the first step to creating a world of love.

Think about it: When the very organ that is critical to life is associated with love, what does that tell us? It tells us that love is *also* critical to our existence. Without it, we are hollow and only shells of the people we can be. Love is our soul, and when we, as individuals and as humanity, accept this and move towards it, great things will transpire.

You cannot contain love; you can only block it or let it flow.

I prefer to let it flow.

Chapter 7
When Mishaps Come Calling

We are not robots. Sometimes we may want to be because our emotional state is too painful or we are too sad, but try as we may, we cannot shut those emotions off. We can numb them or push them deep into a crevice of our soul, but chances are, they will resurface and become un-numbed. I know, I tried, but it never worked. So how do we deal with these negative emotions in a healthy fashion?

Love.

That's right, *love* is the answer.

As I have mentioned, during and since the challenge, I experienced sustained periods of bliss and less stress and have established a pretty solid love-filled disposition. That doesn't mean I don't experience bouts of sadness, annoyance, or fear, but what it does mean is that I suffer these emotions less often and for shorter periods of time. They can still be intense, but now I manage them with affection and go straight to my love toolbox to help me out. Immediately, love starts to flow, lifting me to higher vibrational feelings.

Even without continuing to do all ten love actions daily, I still benefit greatly from the ones I do day to day. The others, I keep in my arsenal of fear-conquering weapons to battle against any bleak moments or to give me a love boost when life throws something in my path that bumps me off the road. It's a given. At some point, things don't work out the way we want, a person annoys us, or a major upheaval such as loss of a loved one or job occurs, and we succumb to feelings of grief, fear, and worry. What I have learnt as I continue to navigate life with my new tools is that simple acts of love will change your world. It is a guarantee, and if you really need a love boost, do a love action geared towards someone else. There is no greater cure to sadness and fear than giving someone love.

Lessons on repeat

As I mentioned in Chapter 4, life will keep teaching you the same lesson until its learnt and cemented in your subconscious so you don't repeat it. I learnt this in my late thirties when I kept dating narcissists until I figured out why and put a stop to it. Even with that, the universe gave me a refresher course and sent one my way in my late forties. He lasted only a few weeks before I saw my pattern re-emerging and nipped it in the bud.

The lesson that I speak of now is one I think many people struggle with, and that is, needing love from someone else in order to feel it. The challenge not only helped me reach new levels of love that surpassed any feelings I had experienced in the past, but it also granted me the wisdom, or so I thought, to no longer depend on love from outside sources. I thought I nailed that lesson, but the universe thought it should give me an opportunity to prove if I did, or if I'd fall back into old paradigms.

I fell back into old paradigms, and honestly, I was shocked at how quickly I let that happen. Why am I telling you this? So you know there's a solution and that it's normal. We are human, after all, and mishaps help us grow.

It happened almost one year after I completed my month of love. There I was, buzzing through life, feeling like I was floating with the clouds—light and vibrant, love-filled and blissful. I carried with me my newfound knowledge, tools, faith, and wonderful connection to Source. I was so immersed in love I felt compelled to share my new lifestyle with friends, especially when they were experiencing times of sadness or fear. I wanted to spread love and let everyone know you don't need anyone else to feel the way I do.

I would say things like, "When your heart is filled with love, there is no room for anguish," and "It's easy, trust me, just do these love actions and watch your life move from sadness to love and bliss."

I'd offer solutions like, "You can't move from sad to glad in one step, but if you introduce more love into your daily actions, your emotions will improve, trust me," and "Remember: you don't need anyone to feel this way, just create the love yourself..."

Blah, blah, blah.

I probably annoyed the heck out of them when they were grappling with a break-up or feelings of profound sadness and stress, and here I was tossing around the L-word like it was so easy to attain! I droned on about how love is the answer for everything and yes, it is omnipresent, but it's up to you to ensure it has a place in your heart.

I meant well, and I know I helped, but it was only after I inadvertently contradicted the very words I spoke and believed that I realised regardless of how love-filled you are, something can enter your life and rock the very foundation you thought was solid. I was riding around on my high horse of love thinking I knew it all when I fell for someone and, two months later, had my heart ripped out of my chest and all my beliefs drained with the tears that poured down my cheeks.

Months after completing my love challenge, I decided it was time to think about bringing romantic love back into my life. Firstly, I thought, I would do the mental preparation and visualise the love and partner I desired. I didn't want to go on the well-known dating apps, and I couldn't go out much, as the pandemic was still keeping people fairly isolated and separated, so figured this was a good place to start. I used my walks with Jeffrey (his walks are so helpful) to fantasise about meeting my perfect mate. I envisioned the perfect life we'd have, his personality and intelligence, his support for my writing, what he looked like, and how he made me laugh.

I repeatedly played in my mind how we met, our first date, and then all the way to us getting married and our wonderful love-filled life together. I had our first kiss on replay and dreamt of all the perfect qualities he possessed. I loved these daydreams and knew that this exercise was getting me in the right mind-frame for dating.

After doing this for a few weeks, I decided it was time to put myself out there. It was the right time to share my love with someone and not just the world. I did some research and chose a paid online dating service. It had a thorough personality test and numerous questions to assist with creating an appealing online profile. I never liked filling in dating profiles, as I find them contrived and somewhat awkward, but I gave this one my best.

To my surprise, only two days after publishing my profile, I started to chat with someone. It was great. He was funny, smart, and local. We agreed to meet for coffee to see how we got on. Well, we got on perfectly, and after date two, we were smitten! Our dates were filled with lots of laughter, we had a lot of similar interests and beliefs, and the physical attraction was definitely present.

I was stoked and very proud of how far I had come. I'd gone from believing I was unworthy of love to filling myself with so much self-love and love for all that I attracted my dream partner. We seemed to be on the same page when it came to what we wanted and were very open with our growing feelings for each other. It was intense and loads of fun.

However, what I thought was exciting, easy, and promising turned into stress and trepidation for him. With no indication or sign of what was to come, he ended it only two months after it began, and my heart fell to new depths. I thought we were enjoying the journey of getting to know each other and loved how seemingly perfect for each other we were. For him, it was too fast and too much. Even though he admitted to driving the pace, he could not keep up with it and pulled the plug.

His reasons were legitimate, and I respected his decision. He needed time to get over his last relationship. He thought he was fine, but as our emotions became stronger, he recognised he was not ready to dive into another relationship yet. He needed to heal, and I had to give him that. We are all on our own journey, and his was walking away from me.

He said he wanted us to try again but didn't know when, nor could he make promises. As much as I wanted to believe we'd be back together, for my own sanity, I had to let him go completely. I was devastated and shocked. I had not suspected a thing and was flabbergasted as to why something so sad was brought into my love-filled life. I didn't get it.

It happened again

Immediately, I closed my heart, put up some walls, and backed myself into a self-pitying, loveless corner of unworthiness. Despite all the work I had done and all the love I felt inside, I went into victim mode and back to old habits. I started questioning what was wrong with me; how could I have been so foolish to believe I'd find romantic love? Here I was, single again, and for the same reason I had heard countless times before: "I'm just not ready for a relationship."

Yet again, another man leaves. The story of my life ...

Frankly, I was shocked by how quickly my beliefs and learnings were thrown into the rubbish. I reverted to my old stories, and instead of fighting them off with the abundance of love I created, I found familiar comfort in my old ways. My new beliefs apparently weren't strong enough yet to withstand the hurt of being dumped one more time. Instead of practicing what I preached about not needing love from anyone else, I got so caught up in his love and our time together, I allowed my feel-good emotions to be controlled by an individual other than myself. I did not follow my own guidance, and my love-filled days became sorrowful. Here I was, a person who claimed to have created a love-filled lifestyle not contingent on others, yet one break-up and I cried for three weeks straight.

This break-up was an eye-opener and a glimpse into how fragile the human psyche can be. I definitely saw how easy it was to revert back to thirty-plus years of behavioural patterns and the impact that such a negative event can have. I was miserable and allowed myself time to grieve, but eventually the pull to feel better became stronger, and I could not focus on sadness any longer.

At that point, I began meditating multiple times a day, even if only for a few moments, but always with the same intention: reclaiming my love and strength. Within a few days, I felt much better and introduced another love action back into my routine to lift my spirits and strengthen my resolve of remaining a person of love. I took a journal and wrote down things I loved each day, reminding myself how wonderful life really is.

I started to search for the lessons and gifts this ending provided. One of the first things that came to me was that I obviously still needed help with not requiring outside validation or relying on others to make me feel loved. With that realisation, I took the opportunity to strengthen my resolve for feeling love regardless of any outside influences.

During my healing process, I took great comfort and solace in one decision that presented itself to me while I was partaking in a luscious, luxurious love moment. I made a conscious choice to change the vernacular I used when describing how I felt about my many failed romances and any future romantic endeavours.

I remember sitting in my living room when he came over to end it, and all I kept thinking as he spoke was, *I cannot keep giving pieces of my heart away. I just can't*. This stuck with me, and in one of my very long, hot, soul-soothing showers, it dawned on me that I don't have to give any of my heart away. In fact, my heart is mine and mine only. It is not for anyone else to have a chunk of; no, it is whole and complete and belongs to me. However, I will *share* it.

That simple change in words from *give* to *share* changed my mindset and filled my heart with all those tiny pieces I thought had been floating in the ether of *exes*. What a relief to feel the wholeness of my heart and know it wouldn't be fragmented again.

Love and learn

Feeling better, I pondered the next set of questions that came to me while licking my wounds. *How did I allow myself to become so attached to how he made me feel? Why did I end up relying on him to feel loved?* These weren't easy questions, and I allowed myself to feel the sadness and hurt as I dug around for answers.

What came to me was that as humans, we have basic needs to feel love, and for all our lives, we are taught that love comes from outside. It is ingrained in us from a young age. All our major love milestones are contingent on being with a partner: first kiss, first love, engagement, marriage, kids, a family living happily ever after. Experiencing these is what we are taught about finding the way to a happy heart and everlasting love.

Just because I found another way to achieve such love by letting love come from me and Source doesn't mean I won't, or can't, feel fantastic because someone shows me love. Rather, I need to recognise that it's only natural and absolutely fine to feel great when someone loves me. What I must practice is not to be attached to their love or reliant on them to supply that love for me. I must practice surrendering and letting go in my relationships—all of them. I must let go of any preconceived ideas of how it is meant to be and just let it be.

I was too attached to an outcome (life partner) that I invented in my head. Now, there is nothing wrong with imagining the outcome you wish that fits into creating your reality with your thoughts. The trick is to not get attached to it and be open to other possibilities.

When I accepted this and realised that what I experienced was completely normal and the important bit is that I learnt from it, I felt a huge sense of relief. Even more important was that I used the tools I created, my love actions, to raise my vibration and get myself back into the loving energy I wished to maintain. I was extremely happy to learn firsthand how helpful these actions were outside of a challenge. You don't need to complete them in the structured format I did for those thirty-one days for them to benefit you; all you need to do is put them into action. One at a time, two at a time, three at a time—it doesn't matter. Just do love and love will flow.

My love journey began the night I walked into the pole, and it will never end. There will be more twists and turns and beautiful outcomes as I continue to grow love and spread it as far as I can. New and old lessons will be presented, and

I will work through them with love, faith, and the tools I now carry with me constantly. This is life.

When I first uttered the words *I am love* several years ago, the freshness of them brought joy. As I evolved and sought an existence contingent on love, speaking those words lost power because I no longer trusted their truth. I needed more than words. I needed to put the words into action and prove to myself that what I said was factual. Am I really love? This is why I created the Full-On Love Challenge, to put those words to the test and prove to myself I can create a life I love.

The challenge surpassed my expectations, and I passed my test. Love became ingrained in my operating system, and now when I repeat the words "I am love," I smile because I *know* it is true. Read on to see how this can become your way of life too.

Part Two

A Love Toolbox

Your instructions for creating a lifestyle of love and experience lasting bliss, unshakeable faith, crazy-ass manifesting, and all-around good vibes.

Chapter 8

Doing Love is the Way to Go

These ten simple acts of love have the power to shift your reality and improve our world. I continue to use them—some daily, some when I need a love boost. I can pick and choose the love actions that will work the best at the time (see Appendix II for ideas), and as soon as I put them into action, I feel better.

Simply by *doing* love.

Some of these, you will recognise from Part One, whereas others will look or sound new. Even if they were not mentioned in previous chapters, they all played a significant role in creating who I am now. Without these ten actions, I could still be wallowing in fear more often than I'd like. These simple acts of love had a profound impact on my life, and I hope they will for you too. Even if you only do a few on a daily basis, your life will change for the better.

Below, you will find a brief description of each of the ten actions and a few tips on how to introduce them into your day. The details for completing the Full-On Love Challenge, along with guidelines for three mini-challenges I put together for you, are in Chapter 9.

1. Hug Yourself

Over the 31 days, I gave myself 154 hugs. That is an average of 4.96 hugs per day. I know it may seem strange to hug yourself, but once you get over that initial awkwardness of wrapping your arms around you and squeezing, the weirdness abates. Or not, and you just accept that it is OK to be a bit weird sometimes.

I'm all right with it.

Hugging carries multiple benefits, regardless of whether you are hugging yourself or someone else. Foremost, it is an act of love and caring, and it feels great. That is why I included it as one of the love actions. I started hugging myself one morning many years ago when I had the urge to wrap my arms around me and tell me how I awesome I was.

Being a person of action, I did it. I loved it so much I did it the next day, and the day after, and the day after that. It went on, and I have not missed a day since. In fact, I now hug myself multiple times a day, just because it makes me feel so good.

It is simple, takes no time, and can be repeated throughout the day. It releases oxytocin and endorphins that increase feelings of comfort and security. It can increase the production of serotonin and dopamine, both of which can relieve feelings of depression or sadness, as well as feelings of loneliness. These same chemicals are released when you hug yourself. I know because I feel it. I am proof.

Try it. Give yourself a hug now!

Another amazing thing about hugging yourself is that it is super easy to send that hug to someone you love, living or not. As I mentioned previously, I mentally hug one of my best friends in Canada regularly, and it feels great! I've also sent hugs to my mum before and after she passed, as we lived so far apart. I can almost smell her perfume when I hug myself and focus on my mum.

How to feel comfortable with hugging yourself

If hugging yourself is too much to fathom at this point and you don't think you're quite there where you can bundle your arms around you and give yourself a squeeze, then start with simply stroking the tops of your hands. Then you can move up and down your arms. Give yourself some nice pats like you are stroking a dog or a cat. Enjoy the sensation of touch on your skin. Feel the softness or the callouses.

Now, while doing this, think loving thoughts. They could be about how good it feels to be touched, or how you love the feeling of your skin, or they could be directed to someone else if that is easier. Once you feel comfortable with that, try a hug. All that entails is clasping your body or arms and squeezing, just as you would anyone else.

2. Meditate

If I had to pick one love action that had the biggest impact on my life, it has to be meditation. It woke me up to a beautiful life and propelled my love journey forward. I chose to do the same guided meditation for the thirty-one days. It is recorded with background music and sounds set to a frequency of 528 Hz—the same frequency that love is postulated to vibrate at. The meditation is produced by Rising Higher Meditation and called "Align with the Frequency of Wellness 528 Hz (Positive Vibration Meditation)." I found it on YouTube. You do not have to do this meditation, though. Please do what feels best for you.

How to introduce meditation into your day

Meditate once daily for three to five minutes. Start slowly if it is brand new or if you have only flirted with meditation and are uncertain or intimidated. The last thing I want to do is scare you from trying it again and make you lose the momentum of doing it daily.

You can find guided meditations online for free if that helps you focus, or you can go to a class, download a meditation app,[6] or sit quietly in stillness focusing on your breath. Do what feels right, and do it daily. You can also visit my website (www.colindalatour.com) to find some meditations I have created.

Try to practice at the same time daily. First thing in the morning is ideal because of the calm state of your mind. If that is not practical, do it when it is and make it a routine.

Make it nice. Sit on a comfy chair, lie down, or sit cross-legged, whichever works. Make sure you are warm, and do not worry about fidgeting or sneezing or anything like that. There is no pressure. It is simply an exercise of going inside and being quiet. Regardless of what mode of meditation you choose, it is important to calm your breathing, focus on your inhales and exhales, soften your eyes or close them to remove unnecessary outside stimuli, and be patient.

Once you are comfortable with five minutes, increase the duration to ten, to fifteen, and once you are comfortable with that, you can meditate longer if you wish. Doing it consistently is the key to forming a habit, and at some point, you won't want to miss a day because of how marvellous it feels. It is such a simple way to love yourself. The proven physical and mental benefits provide great love for your mind and body, and your connection to your higher self strengthens.

Have a play with a few different types, and do not feel disheartened if it takes some time to settle on a method or type you prefer. When you start from a place of willingness

---

[6] There are a number of well-known and respected apps, too many for me to list. I do not use them so cannot provide a recommendation. Reviews or trying them for a period of time can help.

to find a technique you like and a duration that fits into your schedule, it won't be intimidating at all; it will be exciting and fun. Honestly, my take on meditation is, do what works for you and helps you relax the most. Does it feel good? Do you look forward to it? Do you feel great afterwards? Then do it that way.

On some days, I meditated more than once, resulting in a count of forty-one meditations throughout the month. When I doubled up on the days, it was often because I had a question I could not answer or an issue I could not resolve. I would ask my inner guide and meditate on it. I do this regularly and have always received an answer. It may not come immediately or during the meditation, but it will follow.

3. Heart Breath

What I call *Heart Breath* or *Heart Breathing* is a technique I have adapted from the HeartMath Institute. What I do is, every morning and sometimes throughout the day, I slowly and calmly breathe in and out with my hands over my heart and focus my breathing on moving into and out of it. On the inhale, I breathe into my heart, and on the exhale, my breath flows from my heart and through my body while I send love and compassion and healing energy with the breath. The idea is to put your body and mind into congruence with your heart so your physical and emotional bodies are one and come from love.

I did this seventy-seven times during the challenge, and I still do it multiple times daily. It is such a simple tool to quickly put you in a peaceful and loving energy; all you need is breath and focus. It only takes seconds. These are the reasons I love this exercise so much: it is fast, easy, and can be done anywhere to help you feel love and calm your nerves. Deep breaths on their own are very calming and helpful, but coupling them with sending loving thoughts and feelings throughout your body whilst breathing through your heart will amplify your wellbeing.

How to breathe through your heart

Start by taking three to five deep, slow breaths, and focus the flow of it originating from and ending in your heart. Try to feel the breath entering and exiting your heart and spreading throughout your body. Do this at least once a day when you have a quiet minute or two. If it helps, place your palms on your heart to help focus on that location.

Once you have the hang of that, introduce love and gratitude into your breathing. Picture in your mind love coursing through your veins being carried with the oxygen you breathe in. Maybe it looks like small hearts floating downstream moving through your arteries, veins, and capillaries, or maybe it's a sensation, warm and tingly as gratitude, that pulses throughout your body. Or perhaps it is words, such as *I feel love*, that you hear. Whatever it is, let the love and appreciation travel through your heart as you breathe deeply.

4. Love in the Mundane

This exercise is more about loving the moment than yourself or others. It is meant to introduce love into daily actions that you do regularly, such as washing your hands or dishes. Whatever action is a repetitive, almost unconscious action, try to feel love when you are doing it. Imagine what you could possibly love about it and feel gratitude for that. Enjoy it; relish it.

I chose this action because I wanted to take those unconscious actions we do throughout our day and turn them into ones that are filled with love. I figured that if I can feel love while scrubbing my toilet or washing the dishes, I can feel love doing anything.

My two favourite mundane actions during the challenge were washing my hands and washing the dishes. Years ago, while I was taking a yoga teacher training course, the swami described how to bring love into daily practices off and on the mat. As an example, she described feeling the warmth of the water on your hands and feeling the softness of the bubbles as you wash dishes. This resonated with me, and I did it periodically throughout my life thereafter. During the challenge, I did it every time I washed dishes or my hands.

Feeling love for acts such as this will change your perspective. Instead of having bored or resentful thoughts about scrubbing the dishes yet again, I relished that I had warm clean water with fresh-smelling, environmentally friendly dish soap to make the action so enjoyable. Now I actually look forward to washing up and have made it a habit to do it with love on the brain. Bringing love into the banal helped cement love into my way of being. It became the norm when it became part of my everyday activities.

Introducing love into the mundane

Start with activities you already love. If you love cooking, throw more love into chopping those vegetables. If you love brushing your teeth, smile extra-wide and feel blessed you have dental hygiene at your fingertips. Love what comes easily in day-to-day actions. Then you can start introducing love into those actions which are neutral—things you neither love nor dislike, but that are there during your daily life.

If you are impartial about picking your outfit for the day, put some loving feelings into your wardrobe as you caress the fabrics and imagine how good you will feel wearing the clothes you choose. Or if you could care either way about washing the dishes, then feel the luxury of warm, clean, soapy water and be grateful for the meal you just ate from them.

You get the idea—introduce love into any humdrum activity that could use it!

5. Luscious Luxury Love Moments

When I created this love action for the challenge, I thought it would be easy. I was wrong. It was one of the most challenging items to check off my daily list. These were actions that were meant to make me feel lush and blissful, and yet I put them behind all the other love actions. So what are they?

Luscious Luxury Love Moments (LLLMs) are things you do for yourself or to yourself that make you go, "Mmmmm, I love this. This feels delectable." It's that extra-long hot bubble bath while sipping on bubbly, or a sweet yoga session where you do all your favourite poses. Maybe it's a drive in your car with the sunroof open and music blasting, or it could be as simple as a cuddle with your dog, cat, kid, partner … whoever makes you feel good.

LLLMs are all about treating yourself with love. They are about putting yourself first for a moment (or more) and doing something purely to make yourself feel good. They are designed to raise your vibration and encourage you to feel love for yourself, because if you can take the time to treat yourself not once but three times a day, that is a downpour of love, and you deserve it.

When I noticed on day three that LLLMs were some of the last love actions I did every day, I pondered why that might be. It didn't take long to realise that part of it was because *luscious* and *luxurious* are two words that were not very common in my vernacular, but with this challenge, I changed that. I learnt that it's OK to treat yourself regularly. It doesn't have to be expensive or time-consuming; it can simply be five extra minutes cuddling in bed before you swing your feet out to start another day.

The other reason I was finding these difficult was because I still put myself behind everyone else—classic people pleaser. It was still much easier to give love to others before myself, besides all the self-love I had created. After I noticed this, I made a concerted effort to complete two of my LLLMs earlier in the day instead of coming home from the evening dog walk, looking at my checklist, and asking, "OK, three luscious things, hmmm, what can I do in the next couple hours?" I made the decision to put loving myself first, and after a few days of this, I felt the difference.

It was the deliberate repeated action of doing something special just for me that made loving myself even more of a priority. I put loving me first and didn't worry about loving others in these moments. These were just for me—special moments that emphasised the importance of making myself a priority. This challenge never stopped giving; I grew every day, and the onslaught of love provided an abundance of lessons.

During the challenge, I completed about ninety-three LLLMs. Despite the block early on, they became one of my favourite things during the month. Long hot showers with music blaring was one of my favourites. It was such an indulgence to regularly treat myself and never feel guilty about it!

Create your LLLMs

Take three actions that you like or love already, and when you do them, buff them up with a bit of luxury—anything to make the moment feel more special than it already is. For example, if there is a television program you love to watch, maybe give yourself one of your favourite snacks to enjoy as well. Plump up the pillows and lean into them, or cuddle under a soft blanket that feels velvety while you watch. Or do something you have always wanted but were nervous about treating yourself to. Ignore the nervousness and go for it. For example, if you have always wanted to take cooking lessons, go for it.

LLLMs are all about you and what makes you feel really good. Think about those things and put them into action *daily*. Give yourself the right, without guilt, to smile purely because of the decadence you are bestowing upon yourself. You won't regret it.

6. Affirmations and Mirror Work

We have spoken about these earlier, so I will not repeat myself, but they had such a lasting impact I had to include them in my challenge. Both are strong transformational tools that help diminish the negative chatter in your mind and replace it with love and kindness.

Speaking affirmations fills your mind with loving, positive statements that can retrain your thoughts and beliefs. The negative self-talk diminishes as your new thoughts are repeated and become your reality. It may take a while, as you may have been filling your brain with negative babble for years. Be patient and know it is working.

Affirmations to get you started

- I am worthy.
- I can do anything.
- My life keeps getting better and better.

Statements of love and encouragement said in the mirror are especially powerful. Looking into your eyes, your soul, and voicing wonderful things about yourself, in my opinion, is life-changing. The mirror is your immediate response to these statements as it reflects your emotions and reactions back to you and provides a visual cue as to how much you agree with the statements.

Some people may find it difficult, but I urge you to try it and keep trying until it feels good. If it doesn't feel good when you begin, start with something that does, like these statements:

- I am ready to love me.
- I know I am loveable.
- I have so much love to give, I can give some to me.
- What do I love about me?

I especially love the last one: *What do I love about me?* Asking this question prompts your brain to respond automatically with all sorts of fabulous things about you but does not add stress if you have difficulty saying those three little words. It is a great way to open your heart to being more accepting and loving towards yourself.

If you have practiced this for a while, or used the other affirmations above to get you to the point where you find it easy to say "I love you" as you stare into your eyes, try it every time you pass by a mirror or see your reflection. Say it as often as you can and as often as you want—and remember: you don't need a mirror to say "I love me!"

I repeated multiple affirmations in the mirror on eighty occasions over the thirty-one days and still have bits of paper on my walls, my computer monitor, and by my bedside so I am continuously prompted to speak well to myself.

7. Letting Go/Surrender

This one is huge, and as you are aware, it played a starring role in setting up my year of celibacy and retelling the childhood stories that influenced my love life so much. Knowing that we need to free up space to let new stuff in, I had to make this part of the challenge. I had to make room for all the love that was going to pour in.

We can only hold so much in our head and heart. Therefore, we must release the things that do not serve us in order to make space for the things that do. I released or surrendered something daily. It is now a practice that I do when needed.

During the challenge, I let what I should release come to me naturally. It often arrived when I was on my dog walk. I would be walking along, and it would pop into my head: *Colinda, today you should release this.* Or, *perhaps surrendering to this will help you with this ...* Once I knew what I was releasing, the next step was to decide how to release it. Sometimes it was enough to simply say, *I surrender* or *I release you*. Other times I was more creative.

Play with these ideas

If you are not aware of any limiting beliefs you have, or you do not feel a need to let go of anything, start with releasing physical things to make space. Have a declutter session and put all the items you are ready to donate or sell to one side. Then each day, release one of those items symbolically before actually getting rid of it.

During this act of physical release, pay attention and see if anything does come up in your thoughts and emotions that could use mental decluttering—things you no longer want to focus on that have been causing anxiety or worry. Or maybe it was a way you reacted earlier in the day that you didn't like, and you want to remove it from your energy. An easy method for releasing is to write things down, then tear them up or burn them, or simply throw them in the trash. What is important is, you get rid of them. Again, the physical act of release will help cement it in your mind and heart.

For surrendering, that comes from within. It is a willingness to give up some control and trust that no matter what happens, it will all work out and is for the best. This takes some faith, as mentioned, but can simply be faith in the act of surrender.

Both of these actions are essential in your journey. There is no way you can progress without giving up some old ways and thought patterns.

8. Sending Love

This was one of my favourites. It consisted of performing five or more acts of love towards individuals, groups of people, nature, and inanimate objects. Initially, I decided that at least three of the acts of love had to be directed at someone or something else, but some could be for me. However, I noticed right from the start that all of them were directed at others. So I kept it like that.

A lot of these actions were directed at friends and family, and mostly consisted of me sending a loving message in whichever format would reach them. It was a lot of fun. I'd randomly pick people, whoever popped into my brain, and would text, call, or leave a voice message about how awesome they are and that I love and appreciate them. It only took a few moments but had lasting effects, not only for how great these messages made me feel to send them but for the people on the receiving end too. It was so much fun!

Another act of love I did regularly was send love to the people I encountered on my walks or bike rides. I would imagine love pouring out of my heart and streaming directly into theirs as a beam of energy, like I described in Chapter 6. This energetic experience was beautiful and expansive, and I felt the love I was transmitting.

This love action brought so much love to me I was flabbergasted. Not only did I feel love because I was doing loving things, but I received so much love in return from the people I sent it to. One of my friends, who was at home with her husband and two young girls (and could not go anywhere or see anyone during the pandemic because her husband was high-risk), told me that on a particularly rough day, the message I texted her expressing my love for her and our friendship turned her day around and filled her heart with gratitude. It shifted the way she saw things, and she knew life was OK and she would be all right. She was loved.

It is such a simple thing to do and so rewarding for everyone involved. It gives me goosebumps even thinking about it. Messages of joy, love, and kindness should be the norm and sent with abandon.

Wonderful ways to send love

Make it easy. Put a loving note in your child's lunch bag, call a friend just to say I love you, or write your partner a love letter and put it where they are guaranteed to see it.

These are all things we do in our daily lives anyway once in a while. Why not take it up a notch and do it daily? It is easy, joyous, and rewarding. You will notice the love returned after your first act. And why not mix it up? How about sending love to someone you do not know? On your commute to work, send love to the people sitting in traffic around you. Or let a stranger in the line behind you at the coffee shop who is in a rush go ahead of you with love.

Next, when you are really starting to feel how awesome this is, start experimenting a bit more and send love to strangers far and wide. Send love to groups of people or whole populations who are suffering. Expand your love to include all those people and things in the world who need it. Send love to the children with cancer, to the animals dying because of deforestation, or to the land that is dry and parched and will not produce the crops we need.

Send love where there is none, where the world needs it most. This could be to the neighbour who is suffering from dementia or to the countries and people who suffer in the face of war. Open your heart as wide as it can get and send love to the whole Earth. Let your love be carried with the winds as we all become global love generators.

9. Things I Love

I adapted this love action from the self-appreciation journal I spoke about in Chapter 2 where I wrote down all the things I accomplished and appreciated about me. For the challenge, I wanted to expand it to anything I appreciated and loved instead of focusing only on me. I didn't rule out including things I love about me but thought it would be fun to see if I could come up with 310 different things.

Each day, I wrote or drew ten things I loved. These ranged from cooking to unicorns to people in my life. I had a big piece of paper on my wall and added to it daily. I made sure I had pencils, crayons, and pens next to the paper so it was easy to do, and I could add to it when I walked by. I really enjoyed watching the poster-sized lists of items grow.

I tried to avoid duplication, but some things I loved so much just found their way onto the list a couple of times. I replaced them with new ones when tallying up my items at the end of the challenge, only because I wanted to fulfil my desire to have 310 unique items.

This love action is about focusing on all the things you love, so it is a great way to make you feel fantastic, because your attention is focused on the positive. It can also give you further insight into who you are. You may be surprised at some of the stuff you love when you are on day twenty and digging deep to find those items. It was certainly a peek into my personal life (you can find my love items in Appendix I). These items will tell a unique story of who you are as you peruse and review the list as it grows. I cherished that route of discovery.

How to tell your unique love story

I recommend you take time on this love action. Have fun with it, and if you get stuck, get specific. Instead of saying, "I love shoes," say, "I love black, sexy heels." Instead of, "I love travelling," draw a picture of you on a helicopter flying over mountains. This way you will never run out of things you love. The more specific you get, the more options and insight you will have.

You can do as I did—put a large piece of paper on the wall and add to that each day—or you can type them and save them on your computer, or write and draw them in a journal. The important thing is to list ten items daily and try to keep them different. Enjoy what you discover about yourself, and don't be shy about what you write down. You don't have to share it with anyone. To see a picture of my "things I love" poster, you can visit my website (www.colindalatour.com).

10. Loving Kindness Meditation

I hope you don't read *meditation* and think, *What, another meditation? Twice in one day? Are you crazy? I don't have time for this* ... If you are thinking this, don't worry. It's not like other meditations. It can take as little as a few seconds but still have lasting effects.

I first did this meditation about three years ago and loved it. I introduced it into my daily morning practice approximately two years ago. I was reading a book on loving kindness, and it spoke about sending love outward, starting with yourself and expanding from there. This idea spoke to me, and from the very first time I tried it, I was hooked.

Every morning when I do this, it is slightly different. It depends on how I want to send love out that day. Sometimes I spread it across the world, continent by continent; other times, I start with my household, then my family, friends, co-workers, strangers on the street, people in need, those in war zones, those affected by famine, patients in hospitals and their carers, until I include everyone and beyond. More recently, I have added all creatures and all beings in all dimensions.

Traditionally, this includes sending love to those you have difficulties with or to people—and this can be groups of people—with whom you feel some aversion, anxiety, or anguish. This allows for the true nature of love to shine through, as it is inclusive. It isn't discriminating or judgemental but rather accepting and has the power to heal and change lives. It changed mine, and sometimes sending love to those who we think least deserve it helps us just as much as it can help them. Injecting love into any circumstance is beneficial.

Giving love to others through thought

When you do this, it's ideal if you can take a few moments to be quiet, but it's not necessary. It can be done anytime and anywhere; the only things you need are your breath and your imagination. The idea is, you spread your love wider and wider every time you exhale. Take a deep breath in, and as you breathe out, send love and well-being to an expanding circle of people, places, and creatures.

It does not matter specifically how you spread love outward. What is important is the intent and that you feel the love you are sending. If you find it difficult to feel the love, think about someone or something you love unconditionally and feel that, then apply that feeling to this activity. You can sit or lie down, place your hands over your heart to draw your attention to that area of your body, and breathe deeply. On the exhale, spread your love.

Simple and fast.

Or you can take longer. It simply depends on what you decide your practice will be.

If you feel uncomfortable sending love to people you do not know, focus on those you do for now. Then, each time you try it again, broaden your love circle a tiny bit, even if it only reaches the border of your town or city. You may not know everyone in that circle, but you know you all have something in common. As you become more comfortable with this love action, increase your boundary and send it as far and wide as you can.

I found this love action one of the simplest and most rewarding. It took very little energy. I could do it whenever and as often as I wished and felt great peace and joy knowing I was sending out loving energy to so many people. I do it every morning and treasure those few moments of love coursing through my body and out to the world. It feels impactful, and it is a marvellous way to start my day.

There you have it—the ten love actions I did daily for thirty-one days. I will dive into the logistics and how-to aspects next, but for now, bask in the love you created simply by reading about them. These may seem like a lot to do every day, but they aren't. As you introduce them into your daily life as part of one of the mini-challenges, or by jumping in head first and doing them all in the thirty-one-day Full-On Love Challenge, you will see how quickly they become part of who you are: love.

Chapter 9

Now is the Time to Do Love

It's time to put love into action and create a phenomenal life of love. I hope you take the time and energy to complete some, or all, of these challenges and benefit from increased love. They are guaranteed to provide positive results, and I hope you do not view the love actions as arduous tasks but rather opportunities to live in love, always.

I originally didn't consider creating mini-challenges, but when I was telling a friend about the Full-On Love Challenge and doing ten actions per day for thirty-one days, his response ("What? That's too many! How could you find the time?") convinced me that perhaps my level of enthusiasm and commitment was not possible for everyone. Hence, I came up with three mini-challenges that each last a week and only have a few love actions to do each day.

At the same time, I realised it was a great opportunity to provide you with challenges that were geared towards specific love themes. This way, you could pick one that was most meaningful, or do them in an order which may naturally expand your notions and feelings about love in the right order for you. I decided on the three main themes that are present within the Full-On Love Challenge and that the ten love actions apply to:

- self-love

- just love
- spread love.

I also created a Love Action Matrix where you can pick and choose which love actions you want to do and see which theme or mini-challenge they apply to. This allows you to select whichever you feel will fit your love needs at the time.

I found, personally, that whenever I was feeling down, the love actions that focused on sending love out to others especially helped increase my vibration and level of love. You can find the matrix in Appendix II and on my website.

Please do not be dissuaded if you find some of the love actions difficult. Remember: these are challenges and are bound to push you. This is a good thing. If you are like me, you will see this as an opportunity to improve and learn about yourself. When you do find a love action challenging, look inside and see if you can pinpoint why. Take some time to reflect or do one of the love actions that may help, such as surrendering and letting go. Or ask yourself why you find this difficult and meditate on it. Considerate contemplation allows for growth and change.

As you complete the actions and progress throughout the days, you may also notice certain trends. Pay attention to them. Remember on day three when I observed that I was leaving the Luscious Luxury Love Moments (LLLMs) to the end of the day? I kept putting them off, and they ended up being last-minute and not as luxurious or luscious as they could be. When I noticed that, I took some time to reflect on why I struggled with completing this particular activity.

That was when I realised I found it easier to give love to others before giving love to myself. I took this titbit of newfound knowledge and changed my behaviour. After, I made sure that at least two LLLMs were complete before the evening, put more thought into them, and enjoyed them even more.

I find the daily journaling and video recordings of my feelings and observations are still helpful. They provide me with pieces of wisdom that I learnt along the way and can now refer to when I need a reminder. I learnt so many lessons and exciting new things, reforming beliefs and creating a life I truly love. The Full-On Love Challenge changed me and my life.

Timing

The order of how and when you do these activities is entirely up to you. For me, there were certain actions I did as part of my morning routine, and the rest I scattered throughout the day and into the evening, right up to bedtime. The ones I did in the morning were already part of my morning routine, so it made sense to keep them there; also, some of them were easier earlier in the day when my head is clearer.

For instance, a state of meditation is simpler to achieve when you first wake up and before your thoughts are full of the day ahead. I love starting my day with as much loving energy as possible, so besides my daily meditation, I would also complete (and still do) the loving kindness meditation and heart breath all while cosy in bed, basking in its comfort and the delight of my night's sleep. If I felt like repeating them later, I would at a time that felt right—which was the same for all the other love activities. I scattered them throughout my waking hours, changed it up sometimes, and for the most part, fell into a routine of when I did them and in which order.

A typical full-on love-filled day

This is roughly the order that I completed the love actions, with multiple acts randomly repeated throughout the rest of the day.

First, I'd meditate using the same one I mentioned in Chapter 8 for the thirty-one days. Next, I would do my heart breathing and hug myself a few times. My endorphins flowed before I even got up. After, I would send love out with the Loving Kindness Meditation.

Then, I would swing my feet to the floor and do some yoga. Though not part of the love challenge, it is something I do every morning and find very beneficial to my overall state of being. Once done with yoga (or shaking; see the day four excerpt in Chapter 10 for why I love shaking my body), I would walk to a mirror and say "I love you." Normally, that was followed by a mundane activity like washing my hands and focusing on how great the warm water felt and how I loved the fresh smell of my hand soap.

By that time, it was almost the start of my work day, so maybe I would sneak a loving message to someone and a look in the mirror as I brushed my teeth to repeat some of my other favourite affirmations. If I hadn't done a LLLM yet, I'd make sure two were done before mid-afternoon, one of them often being a very long, steamy shower in which I would sip on a coffee, one of my all-time favourite activities and in the top three of LLLMs on this challenge.

On my lunch break, I'd send the remaining love messages to people and write down or draw a few things I loved as part of the Things I Love action. I'd add to this throughout the day and, as mentioned, had it on my wall so I could see the items easily. It was fun to see all the things I loved and a great reminder about how awesome my life was.

Love in the Mundane was repeated each time I washed a dish or my hands, or found some other routine that could use a love injection, such as making my bed. Inevitably, on my evening walk with Jeffrey, an idea would come to me about what I needed to release. But this wasn't always the case. Something to surrender could pop into my head at any time. I would then decide how to release it and go from there.

Sometimes, I would simply say "I release you" at that moment. Other times, I would perform a meditation to release it (yep, another meditation) or write it down and burn the piece of paper. Whatever my intuition told me to do, I listened.

As you can see, there is no definitive order to the love actions; rather, a routine will make itself known to you as you complete them. You will find the best way to fit love actions into your day, and soon they will become a habit.

The beauty of the challenges

All the challenges can be done by anyone and anywhere. You do not need anything except yourself, a pen and paper or computer, and the desire to love.

As mentioned, if you find doing ten love actions for thirty-one days daunting, select one of the mini-challenges first. Choose the one that speaks to you the most. I recommend doing all of them, and when you are ready to immerse yourself in love for a month, try completing the Full-On Love Challenge.

It was with this challenge that I achieved the results I recorded and ended up doing more than the minimum requirements because it felt so good. I even added extra love actions, like sending love into the houses where Jeffrey stopped on our walks.

No worries if you don't do extra. The important thing is to do the acts daily for the duration of the challenge and the minimum number for each. If you do want more, you can repeat these challenges as often as you like. Spread the love by inviting your friends and family to try. You can make a game out of it; see who can do the most love actions in the shortest period of time.

Or use the Love Action Matrix to select love actions to give to your friends or partner to try. You can do that for each other and feel the love grow around you. The possibilities are endless, but the end result is the same: more love in your life and all the wonderful side effects that go along with it.

How to get started

1. Pick a challenge (see the following section).
2. Pick a date to start. Keep in mind that you'll need one week for the mini-challenges and one month for the full-on challenge.
3. Go to my website (colindalatour.com) and download the Love Action Checklist for your challenge. Or you can create your own; visit Appendix II for an example.
4. Set up reminders to do each love action throughout the day. You can use your phone, an alarm, timer, or just the checklist to remind yourself of the actions you need to do as you check them off. You can do several in one go, or spread them out throughout your waking hours. Obviously, the action Love in the Mundane will be done when your mundane actions are completed.
5. Find something to record your thoughts and reflections on. You can write them in a journal, type them into your computer, or video/audio record yourself. Don't skip this step. It is beneficial to document how you are feeling and things you notice as the challenge progresses. I highly recommend taking time each day to do this, even if it's only a few lines or words in a voice recording.

6. Jump in full-heartedly and be open to possibilities.
7. Love yourself when you miss an action or forget a day. Reflect on why or how you missed it, then carry on.
8. Reward yourself throughout, and at the end, celebrate your accomplishment.

The challenges

Here are some recommendations and requirements, as well as a description of the different challenges. Each challenge follows the same instructions listed above, points 1 to 8.

Some of the minimum requirements are different in the mini-challenges compared to the full one. This is because those love actions are geared towards the specific theme of the mini-challenge, and I wanted to make sure you really felt the love.

Full-On Love Challenge

This challenge is the original love challenge, the one I created during the writing of this book and described in Chapter 5.

Instructions

Do all ten love actions listed below daily for one month. If you need, refer to Chapter 8 for more information and help on how to do the love actions. I recommend completing at least the minimum number required (most are just one a day) to get the results I did, but ultimately, this is up to you.

Love actions

1. Hug Yourself—1 time per day
2. Meditate—1 time per day
3. Heart Breath—1 time per day
4. Love in the Mundane—3 times per day
5. Luscious Luxury Love Moments—3 times per day
6. Affirmations and Mirror Work—1 time per day
7. Letting Go/Surrender—1 time per day
8. Sending Love—5 times per day
9. Things I Love—10 items per day
10. Loving Kindness Meditation—1 time per day.

Self-Love Mini-Challenge

This challenge focuses on increasing your level of self-love. The love actions chosen for this will help you accept yourself and nourish the seedlings of unconditional self-love that are growing. Do this challenge for a week:

1. Hug Yourself—3 times per day
2. Heart Breath—2 times per day
3. Luscious Luxury Love Moments—3 times per day
4. Affirmations and Mirror Work—1 time per day.

Just Love Mini-Challenge

This challenge focuses on just feeling love. The love is not directed at yourself or anyone else. It is purely to enjoy the feeling of love throughout your day and increase your overall state of love. Do this challenge for a week:

1. Things I Love—write or draw 10 items per day
2. Love in the Mundane—5 times per day
3. Meditate—1 time per day.

Sending Love Mini-Challenge

This challenge focuses on sending love to others and is a great way to bolster how you feel. If you are ever in the dumps, I highly recommend picking this challenge to help you feel fantastic. Giving love to others is a surefire way to get you in a better mood. Do this challenge for a week:

1. Sending Love—5 times per day to people you know, through voice message, text, video, in person, etc.
2. Loving Kindness Meditation—1 time per day
3. Sending Love—3 times per day to people you don't know. You can do this in your head or even by expressing sincere gratitude to someone you encounter.

Living in love

There you have it—four challenges to help you create a love-filled lifestyle. If you commit to any of these challenges, I guarantee it will change your life for the better, as I have yet to meet someone who said they feel awful when doing loving things. Or you can put your trust in me, someone who has completed the Full-On Love Challenge (and the weekly ones multiple times), continues to do about six or more of the love actions daily, and thrives from the love generated. These actions have become part of who I am, and I cannot imagine going a day without doing them.

As you saw in Chapter 7, these actions can have a huge positive impact on your life, even at the darkest times. I am a new person since I introduced these simple acts of love into my daily routine. I live predominantly in a high-vibration state, blissful and carefree, and I bounce back rapidly from any sort of stressful situation. Basically, I accomplished exactly what I sought to do: live a life I love.

Living in Love

You too can create a life you love merely by putting the love actions into, well, *action*. Once you notice how fantastic you feel while doing them, they will become habits, because you will not want to lose that loving feeling. And from these habits, you will develop your own love discipline, which will become your way of life.

That is living in love.

Chapter 10

Raw Results and Lavish Love

When I was doing the Full-On Love Challenge, I wrote a lot and enjoy perusing my thoughts and lessons from those days. Some things I have forgotten but appreciate again when I look back on what I journaled or video-recorded. Other bits I'll never forget, because the feelings and outcomes are still happening as I continue my life of love.

I wanted to share some of the unrefined emotions and things that occurred during those transformational thirty-one days to give you a taste of what occurred in real time. These excerpts will give you a view from the perspective of someone doing the challenge and provide a deeper look into exactly what was going through my head and heart at the time. They also offer some things I did during the challenge that may not be mentioned but I felt were worth sharing here.

I have kept these entries close to the original journal format. Some are raw and lengthy, while others are brief and to the point. They are little snippets of my brain on love and things I hope inspire you.

Day 1
Love is contagious

If I can continuously broadcast love just by being and existing, I am sure doing this would make me love even more. I think love is contagious, just like laughter, smiles, and yawns—if you give love, you are going to get it back.

Imagine if we all vibrated with love, what a different world we would live in. That is my ambition—a world governed by love.

Day 2
Releasing what you do not need

I believe to make space for more love, I need to keep letting go of things that do not serve me. So, this act of releasing is one of the most helpful daily activities, I believe.

Day 3
Spreading love is fun

Really loving the responses I'm getting from sending out love messages as part of my five acts of love. It has been brilliant. If a person comes to mind, I send them a message about how wonderful they are or how much I love them. I dare anyone to try that one day and see how they feel!

Day 4
Shaking up our life

There is nothing like a good shake. It moves our energy around and obviously gets us moving. I do love it and was first introduced to shaking through yoga. I was watching a video on breaking patterns and the exercise of shaking your body was highlighted. It is such an awesome tool to break up monotony and help loosen energy blocks. The randomness of shaking our body whichever way it goes disturbs our normal energy pattern and frees us from attachment.

I love it so much, I shake a lot.

Day 5
Love is a tool for improvement

I am craving more love, which is making me do more love-related actions, but I need to also change my thoughts. I am not a negative person and I love and accept myself, even the bad, but that doesn't stop me from having negative or self-critical thoughts sometimes. More love has made me ready to make more of a concerted effort to change those remaining negative brain networks to positive, loving energy.

It is time.

Day 6
Never underestimate self-love

When we feel love and bliss, we feel lighter, like we are floating on clouds. But when we are sad or angry, we feel heavier and lower. Remember: never underestimate the power of self-love, as it influences how you present yourself to the world and how you cope with life's many events. If you love yourself, you will want to keep this up, because you'll get so used to feeling awesome, you will not want there to be any other feeling!

Living in Love

Day 7
Love is reciprocated

I notice the more I give love, the more I want to give. I want to do more things that show love, that feel like love, and that give love to others and myself. Plus, when I do give love, more comes back to me. It is glorious. It is proof that love creates love.

You cannot win anything with anger and hatred; it has to be love. If you give love, love will be returned. It may not always be immediate but it will be returned. Remember that.

Day 8
Look after yourself and feel good about it

I looked after myself so I could call Mum that night and look after her[7] without feeling drained or depleted. I wanted Mum to feel my love, support, and strength. For me to do that, I had to be full of love, full to the brim, and overflowing with love to give.

It felt right to listen to what I needed and move forward with it. I was a basket case at work and knew it would be better for me to let myself feel, let myself experience the emotions that were bubbling …

The biggest lesson from this day is to look after ourselves, to not feel badly when we take time for ourselves, to relish it and love it, and to be appreciative that we allow ourselves to be nourished and loved. It is one of the dearest gifts we can give to ourselves and others. As I have written before, how can we give love to others if we do not have it to give?

---

[7] My mother had been misdiagnosed with cancer, and I was told the day before. I was calling her that evening to see how she was. She was later properly diagnosed with congestive heart disorder and passed away from a stroke before this book was published.

Day 9
Love never stops growing

On day nine there was another shift. My love feelings wanted more! My inner being said, *Go for more!* Let's give more love, let's do more love, let's be more love! I found myself wanting to perform more of the items, wanting to introduce new things to be in the vibration of love, so I did.

It was truly blissful. I had this voice constantly, lovingly prompting me to do more and feel more love.

Day 10
Love and gratitude

What are some words that come to mind when you think about love? For me, the words *thank you* come to mind, because immediately when something I love comes to mind, I think how grateful I am to have it in my life. For example, if I think about Jeffrey, my dog, I think how thankful I am that he is part of my life, that he is so adaptable and has always been there for me if I am sad or need a cuddle. I am forever grateful he is my dog.

When I think about how I love my home, my friends, my family, I think about how fortunate I am to have all of it. How grateful I am.

Do you see what I'm getting at? Can you think of something you love and are *not* grateful for? Does something like that exist? I can't think of anything. Everything I love, I am grateful for because it brings me joy, peace, bliss ... How can I not be thankful for those beautiful emotions, those high vibrations?

Day 11
Listen to your inner voice, it knows best

Another phenomenon is happening that I touched on before but have not gone into detail about: I am more receptive to my inner being. I hear and feel that voice more, and what is even more important, I am listening to it. I trust it. My trust levels have risen far above what they were. If I get a feeling, a hunch, an idea, thought, nudge, I follow it. I act on these, and so far, they have been right. I noticed this increasing since about day four or so, but it really became evident on day eleven.

I am also cognizant and aware of energies that take me out of feeling good, take me out of that love vibration, and automatically, I want to change it, I want to feel good again.

Day 12
Love and bliss

Introduced more fun into my day today. Skipped, laughed more, sang—did more fun things to bring love into my energy! More bliss brings more love, more love brings more bliss!

Day 13
Treat yourself

Focused on me, as I felt I needed a day of self-love.

When I hugged myself, I thought of me. When Jeff stopped on our walk, I said *I love you, Colinda*. I am so proud and happy that I listened to myself and focused more love on me today. We need to love ourselves; it keeps that loving energy circulating. Plus, it is just nice to treat yourself once in a while, isn't it?

Day 14
Two weeks in and ... pure love

So, today was blissful again. I consciously and unconsciously went into that state of love and alignment with Source. I could do it in a few seconds, and I could notice the changes physically and mentally. My skin tingled, the boundary of my skin faded, and I couldn't always tell where I ended and the universe began.

Then, I could feel a tingle in my brain/head and pure bliss. Such joy and happiness I felt in alignment. I felt pure love ...

I am completely thrilled with the way this experiment is going. It's beautiful and full of surprises. I am in love with everything.

Day 15
Love is only the beginning

I feel as if a bubble of peace has descended around me, and nothing can rouse me from this beautiful, blissful serenity.

I am almost in a meditative state but fully conscious and awake. It has even traversed into my workday. Instead of being in work mode, I am in peace mode. I asked for a solution to not being blissful at work, and my wishes were granted less than twenty-four hours later.

Further proof that manifestation is happening faster because of my raised vibration. I feel like I can take on anything and nothing will bother me. I am at peace with me, my day, my life, the world.

Day 16
Love solves everything

I keep having amazing talks with my mum. That is not common. Yes, they have occurred, and she is very intelligent and we can have great talks, but often calls with her have been a negative source in my life. Generally, I get stressed before I call her for various reasons, but I'm working on this always. And lately, all our calls are wonderful. Regardless that she lost a daughter weeks ago and then was diagnosed with lung cancer, our conversations are filled with love and positivity.[8]

Day 17
Love Should Rule the World

I cannot get over the feelings of peace, tranquillity, and love. The oneness I feel with every breath. It is amazing. From the moment I wake up, I feel this. It is a different sensation I carry around with me now because I am operating at a different vibration. ...

I said to myself, *Let this love challenge spread around the world.* My goal is to help millions by creating more love.

That's what we must do. We cannot just speak of it; we must put it into action in our daily lives so it becomes the vibration we operate at.

Day 18
Love is there no matter how you feel

So, what is the lesson, you may ask? Well, this is when I accept myself no matter how low my vibration. Knowing

---

[8] All my relationships improved during this challenge, and thereafter. Operating from a place of love can solve anything.

that love and bliss are attainable, but maybe not right now, is OK. It is good enough to realise I can get there soon, maybe later today or maybe tomorrow. It doesn't matter. This is a lesson in self-acceptance and loving no matter where you are. I may not feel the high vibration, but that doesn't stop me from being loving to the best of my ability.

The fact that I know I will be in that high vibration state again is good enough for now.

Day 19
Love is more than an emotion

Doing more digging on the sensation of love, I read some interesting pieces about how love is not an emotion but goes beyond that. This, of course, I agree with and have the proof in my challenge. My love actions throughout these past nineteen days have spurred on much more than feeling love, bliss, happiness, or any other emotion up there with the love vibration.

Love has increased my intuition, sped up my manifestations, aligned me with Source, and helped me through times of deep sorrow with grace and positivity.

Love is everywhere and in everything.

Day 20
Do not be scared of discomfort—it means growth

It was a growth spurt, and I was feeling uncomfortable because I was not growing fast enough for my physical reality to catch up with my daydream reality.

I recognise that now. I know when growth spurts happen; I can feel the transformation because there is an element of discomfort. Not every bit of me is expanding at the same rate, so I feel uneasy, off-kilter, sometimes even a bit discombobulated. Now I go with it because it means I am on the right path.[9]

Day 21
Utopia

I wish that everyone every day sent love to someone or to people in need. I want to start a trend where it's cool to imagine love streaming out of your heart and into the hearts of people who walk by, to patients in hospital beds or victims of war.

I want a world where it is normal for love to be thought of as part of the solution and fully integrated into world politics, the economy, our daily lives, education, and the corporate world.

I want to make people understand that love is not weakness, that it is a life-changer, that it improves everything it comes into contact with.

I want people to operate from love, not hatred, judgement, or disdain. I want love to be at the forefront of everyone's thoughts and actions. I want a world filled with people who only love.

Day 22
We are love

We are love—we must remember this. Love is within us, around us, runs through us, and is provided by Source, the very energy that created us, always. We are never unloved. That is impossible.

---

[9] You may notice as you progress through the challenge that you experience levels of discomfort or that you no longer fit into the mould you used to be in. That is because expanding your levels of love will expand who you are, and you need time for your reality to catch up with the new you. This discomfort is a good thing because it means you are growing, and it will pass.

Day 23
Love is who I am

Today has been another love-filled day. I am noticing more and more that love is just part of my day now. It is moving from my conscious awareness to just being part of my existence. Now, without thinking of it, every time I wash my hands, I feel love. Love for the soap, the water, whether or not it warms up before I finish, the fact that I have running clean water …

I am more in tune with Mother Nature than I ever have been. I can feel the shift in season around me as soon as I step into the green; I feel it all. I feel Source, I feel love, I feel the life that surrounds me.

Love is definitely more prevalent in my life. I feel guided by it more. It is becoming my dominant approach.

It is in my thoughts more automatically. It is becoming who I am.

Day 24
The beauty of boundaries

I set boundaries today and did not feel guilty about it. That was a first. I am growing as a person and loving myself even more, recognising the importance of putting myself first and keeping my love bucket brimming and overflowing so I can give that love to others.

But today, I put into action the knowledge that it is OK to say no sometimes when you cannot help someone because you are busy doing something for you.

You don't have to drop what you are doing to be nice and do something because someone asked. No—you can say no when your project comes first. Today, my project, this project, came first, and I said no to someone I never said no to before. Felt good to look out for me.

Day 25
No reason to be shy

I am feeling freer with my actions because they are all from love, so no need to hold back or be embarrassed or shy. What have I got to lose when coming from a place of love? Nothing. Because I am love, I will always be love and I will always feel love. There is no fear anymore.

Day 26
Celebrate yourself often

Today, my friend spoke about celebrating myself for all I have done. I have supported my family as best I can from far away. I have looked after myself under these trying circumstances and started this challenge and writing. I have helped my mum on her journey since diagnosis, which is just fresh and new. I have worked my day job and been supporting others ... She mentioned I have been through a lot and have done a lot; I need to celebrate that.

So I'm going to show myself some more love tonight and celebrate my recent accomplishments! I deserve it, and once in a while—no wait, regularly—we need to celebrate ourselves—our wins, big and small, our accomplishments. Sometimes it's cause to celebrate because we made it through the day unscathed.

Day 27
Spread love through energy

Thoughts are energy, and they carry different energy depending on what they are. Therefore, if I can produce love and light-filled energy and direct it away from me through focused blissful thought, then how could that not alter the surrounding environment? It has to.

Day 28
Complete transformation

Today when I asked myself what I would like to release, it came to me beautifully and peacefully.

"Me."

It is time to release the old me. It makes sense. This past week or more, I have really been feeling my growing pains. I am ready for the new life, the one that comes so easily because it is what I am meant to do.

Releasing the old me does not mean I am forgetting my past and all those in it. It means I am no longer letting it run my life. I am making space for my new life, and those things that are not at my vibration are simply dropping from my reality.

I am ready to let go of the old Colinda and jump into serving a greater good. I am ready to release all my limiting beliefs and step into the courage of being me and living in love.

Day 29
I am love

It has been the same these last few days. I am operating at a high vibration and able to focus easily on love and light.

It is becoming second nature, and I remain in a pleasant disposition.

Day 30
Love is Source, and we are love

What has up to day thirty shown me? It's shown me that love does make a difference ... These exercises over the past thirty days have led to beautiful moments where I am able to connect to Source and feel Source energy flow through my body. Even just a simple breath in, I feel Source, I feel the loving energy, and I remember Source and love are one. Therefore, I can tap into that beautiful, infinite loving Source energy anytime. So grateful!

Day 31
The path of love is always unfolding

I did a lot of loving things for myself today. I am feeling a bit raw that this is coming to an end, but I know it is also just the beginning in a lot of ways. I feel so blessed that this challenge came to me. I see it as a great gift. Things that I did throughout the challenge are now habits. I wash my hands with love every time, smelling the soap and feeling the luxury of warm, clean water. I do my dishes with love, and I feel love in my surroundings.

This journey has been love opening up and continuously unfolding in front of me. Love is present in all my functions throughout the day. Everything I do now is immersed in love.

I feel such gratitude for this challenge and all it has taught me.

Afterword

Becoming a Global Love Generator

If you want to become a Global Love Generator and spread love, join me by performing love actions specifically designed to propagate love. You can visit the Love Action Matrix in Appendix II and select any love action that is marked for spreading love.

Perform some or all of these activities daily and direct your thoughts to specific groups of people, places, creatures, or things that you feel could use more love. This does not need to take a long time; it can merely be seconds of focus. The important thing is to focus your love outward to whom/where/what you want it to reach.

This activity can be done by yourself, or you can increase the love by doing it with others. Convince a friend or family member to join you at a specific time and double the impact by both focusing your loving energy.

For myself, it became fiercely evident as I moved through the thirty-one days that beautiful October that this was my purpose. I have not been the same since, nor do I wish to return to the person I was before I introduced love into my life as a flowing faucet. Loving others is easy. Loving yourself is a bit more challenging. Loving the world is a responsibility we must undertake. It is not hard, nor is it time- or energy-consuming, but it is a necessity for creating a better world for ourselves and our children.

Creating a world that is safe, happy, and love-filled starts with us as individuals. If you take anything from this book, let it be that the act of healing yourself can heal humanity.

Join me as a Global Love Generator and visit colindalatour.com for more inspiration on creating a world of love.

Appendix I

Statistics and Insights

Included in the following statistics are the number of times I did each love action along with some notes if I made any changes to the challenge along the way. I also included what I did for my Luscious Luxury Love Moments, the Things I Love that I wrote for each day, and what I let go of during those thirty-one days.

Please note: I redacted anyone's name or something I considered a wee bit too personal to share.

Hug Yourself
154 times

About halfway through, sometimes when I hugged myself, I started imagining I was hugging specific people and sent that hug to them. On day 17, my friend said she started hugging herself. I was really happy it was spreading.

Meditate
41 times

Heart Breath
77 times

I started doing light breath, too, where I breathed in and out light from Source. I envisioned a golden light pouring into my head or heart, then I'd breathe that light throughout my body and back out into the world.

Love in the Mundane
147 times

Luscious Luxury Love Moments
108 moments

There are definitely some preferred LLLMs in this list! You can use these for inspiration or have a laugh. I did when I counted how many times I "loved myself" in the month.

Day 1

- cuddles with Jeff (my dog)
- wank (don't judge, you will see it is one of my favourite loving things to do!)
- fancy drink

Day 2

- hugged trees
- ordered pizza and ice cream
- napped on the sofa

Day 3

- wank
- morning cuddles with Jeffrey
- tarot cards

Day 4

- shake off
- dancing
- listened to Abraham Hicks
- long hot shower
- wank

Day 5

- blasted music and sang along
- kegels
- more music
- cuddles and played fetch with Jeff inside—so much fun

Day 6

- energy healing
- morning wank
- long hot shower

Day 7

- different morning yoga session
- music in the shower
- beautiful cuddles and fun with Jeffrey

Day 8

- beautiful walk with Jeffrey
- Call with XXX
- walk in the garden

Day 9

- not going to Tesco
- great call with mum
- shaking

Day 10

- shower with coffee
- beautiful yoga
- Netflix binge

Day 11

- shower and coffee
- celebrated Thanksgiving with a friend
- made a feast

Day 12

- shower with coffee
- beautiful walk with Jeffrey
- tea with my friend and her son

Day 13

- kegels, kegels, kegels!
- smelled the roses
- cuddles with Jeffrey

Day 14

- beautiful long hot shower
- quick escape to lie on the mattress in my garden in the sun
- luxurious moment back in bed this morning

Day 15

- cuddles with Jeffrey on the air mattress outside (double whammy!)
- taking a new dog-walking route
- enjoying my flowers

Day 16

- five minutes extra in bed
- lying in the grass
- hugging trees

Day 17

- hands in the sea
- bike by the sea
- yoga
- writing
- wank

Day 18

- wank
- lie in and cuddles with Jeffrey
- nesting—rearranging the dining room—change

Day 19

- cuddles with Jeff
- lying on the mattress outside
- shaking
- longer shower

Day 20

- shot a video and loved it!
- wank
- got info I wanted by asking

Day 21

- time to cry for mum
- dinner at my friend's
- messaging with my cousin

Day 22

- beautiful shower
- extra lie-in this morning
- wank

Day 23

- extra lie-in
- looked for houseplants
- wank
- snuggled on the sofa with my lover

Day 24

- watched Netflix
- loving cuddles with Jeffrey

- shower with coffee
- danced in the shower

Day 25

- wank
- beautiful yoga practice
- smiled riding in the rain
- coffee and music in the shower

Day 26

- played with Jeff
- bought vegan fest VIP ticket
- extra meditation that was so peaceful
- napped

Day 27

- cuddles with Jeff
- wank
- nap and more cuddles with Jeffrey

Day 28

- video call with sisters and mum
- cuddles with Jeffrey
- meditate
- wank

Day 29

- arranging my flowers
- play time with Jeff
- wank

Day 30

- going to Tesco
- wank
- cooking dinner

Day 31

- cuddles with Jeff
- wank
- dancing and singing
- moved my home office and made my home more comfortable

Top Three

- wanks: 15
- long Showers (often with coffee): 13
- cuddles with Jeff: 12

Affirmations and Mirror Work
80 times (in front of a mirror repeating multiple affirmations)

My favourite affirmations:

- I love you/I love me.
- I can do anything.
- I am a bestselling author.
- I am a Global Love Generator.
- I am worthy.
- I am love and light.

Letting Go/Surrender
31 items

I let go of the following:

1. XXX
2. Debt
3. Anguish
4. XXX
5. Dad
6. My childhood
7. Mum
8. Control
9. The end result
10. XXX
11. Negative talk about my body
12. XXX
13. Resentment towards my day job
14. Limiting beliefs about money
15. Judgement (this is ongoing)
16. Pain
17. People who cheated on me or with my partner
18. Fear of having no money
19. Lack
20. XXX
21. Fear of failure
22. Fortieth birthday fiasco
23. Self-judgement
24. All my exes
25. XXX
26. My career
27. Stress in my shoulders and neck
28. The old me
29. Judgement, again and always!
30. Financial burden
31. Outcomes of this challenge

Sending Love
210 acts of love

I added sending love outward whenever Jeffrey stopped on our walks and when my mindfulness bell went off. My mindfulness bell is from an app I downloaded which chimes at random intervals during the day.

Things I Love
310

I tried to remove all duplicates and replace them with unique items when I was tallying them.

Day 1

1. Jeffrey
2. Yoga
3. Receiving parcels
4. Taking videos
5. Scented candles
6. My green knit hoodie
7. Lakes, sea, ocean—water
8. Loud awesome music
9. Vegan ice cream
10. Tattoos

Day 2

1. Unicorns
2. Mermaids
3. Books
4. Rainbows
5. Animals

6. Cake
7. Mixed martial arts
8. XXX
9. Giraffes
10. Coffee

Day 3

1. Mother Mother (my favourite band)
2. Gardening
3. My body
4. Earrings
5. XXX
6. Sunshine
7. Flowers
8. Being on camera
9. Ping pong
10. Kissing

Day 4

1. Pancakes
2. Maple syrup
3. A delicious cup of Earl Grey tea
4. Hot water bottles
5. Incense
6. Dancing in my living room
7. Bubbles
8. Trees
9. Video calls with friends
10. Curling up with a book and a blanket

Day 5

1. Showers
2. Hugging trees

3. Shoes
4. Vegetables
5. Archives
6. Feeling safe
7. Records management
8. History
9. Fluvog shoes
10. Feeling sexy

Day 6

1. Walking in the woods
2. Castles
3. Timber (a childhood pet)
4. My friend's cakes
5. Nine West
6. Vegan hotdogs and milkshakes
7. Listening to the waves
8. My robe
9. Chocolate
10. Me

Day 7

1. Candles
2. Purple
3. Sleeping naked
4. Northern lights
5. Meditation
6. Beach days
7. Hammocks
8. Driving
9. Sex
10. Picnics

Day 8

1. Staying up late
2. Shopping
3. Bookstores
4. Sleeping in
5. Exploring
6. Peanut butter cookies
7. Trampolines
8. Hot tubs
9. Strength
10. Resilience

Day 9

1. My bed
2. Sparkles
3. Helping
4. Cuddles with Jeffrey
5. Smiles
6. A good party
7. Climbing mountains
8. Nutritional yeast
9. Spas
10. Lying on my air mattress in the garden

Day 10

1. Receiving
2. A good sandwich
3. Drinking water
4. Crow pose
5. Cooking for people
6. Beets
7. Giving

8. Bikinis
9. Vegan cheese
10. Pickles

Day 11

1. My lips
2. Entertaining
3. Sparkling snow
4. Thanksgiving
5. Riding in a balloon
6. Decorating for parties and/or holidays
7. Cider
8. Glass of wine
9. Seeing animals
10. A good comedy

Day 12

1. My eyes
2. Cards
3. Friends
4. Birds
5. Erotica
6. Holding hands
7. Random acts of kindness
8. Disco
9. Exercise
10. Walks on the beach

Day 13

1. Bread and vegan butter
2. Sunbathing
3. Playing board games

4. Acting like a goof
5. Road trips
6. Cartwheels
7. Challenges
8. Playing in the snow
9. Spanakopita
10. Sundays

Day 14

1. Gaia TV
2. Yellow mustard
3. Laughing
4. Carrots
5. Slow dancing
6. Dressing up
7. Netflix
8. Spiral staircase
9. Halloween
10. Celery juice

Day 15

1. Morning yoga
2. Kissing Jeffrey
3. Hot springs
4. Wanking
5. Learning
6. Sunny beaches and lounging on a beach chair
7. My cosy comforter
8. Columbine flowers
9. Veganism
10. Peace

Day 16

1. My new Hoover
2. Refrigeration
3. Fridays
4. Camels
5. Pizza
6. Solving problems
7. Punching bags
8. This challenge
9. Researching
10. Ferns

Day 17

1. Weddings
2. Saturday mornings
3. Floating down rivers
4. Chips and mayo
5. Infinity pools
6. Gaia yoga
7. Lilies
8. Christmas trees
9. Making truffles
10. My heart

Day 18

1. Lynx
2. Mushroom adventures
3. Daydreaming
4. Nesting
5. Change
6. Bison
7. Foxes

8. Hedges
9. Wolves
10. Decorating

Day 19

1. Sex in a hot tub
2. XXX
3. XXX
4. XXX
5. Crystals
6. Sex in the shower
7. Skinny dipping
8. Fresh sheets
9. Honest polygamous relationships
10. XXX

Day 20

1. Skate skiing
2. Waterfalls
3. Ancient ruins
4. Sheep
5. Clarity
6. Pigs and all animals
7. Being spanked
8. Amber
9. Sun shining through the windows
10. Running

Day 21

1. Watching nature
2. Bird watching
3. Dinner out
4. Hummus

5. Drinking vegan milk out of a cereal bowl
6. Looking at sparkling snow—almost a duplicate, but not quite
7. Cuddles after sex
8. Canada Day
9. Full moons
10. Visiting friends

Day 22

1. Dates, the fruit
2. All creatures
3. Comfortable clothes
4. Live theatre
5. Willow trees
6. Fortune-telling
7. Sunrise on top of mountains
8. Travelling by train
9. Great Slave Lake
10. Macadamia nuts

Day 23

1. Money
2. Palo Santo
3. Golden light
4. Pushing myself
5. Art
6. Galleries
7. Languages
8. Archaeology
9. Supporting local business
10. Bald eagles

Day 24

1. Monkeys
2. Changing my house around
3. My hair being played with
4. Receiving cunnilingus
5. Natural beauty
6. My period
7. Attention
8. Public speaking
9. XXX
10. Drinking coffee in the shower

Day 25

1. Making art
2. The weekend
3. Vacuuming
4. Sugar
5. Cold pizza
6. No bull burgers
7. Eating
8. XXX
9. Great deals
10. Libraries

Day 26

1. Imagining the best-case scenario
2. Superhero movies
3. Cloud-gazing
4. Jenga
5. My childhood tea cup
6. Fairy lights
7. Self-hypnosis
8. Standing

9. Dressing up sexy for my man
10. Fort Liard hot springs

Day 27

1. Being a Canadian northerner
2. Bananas
3. Massages
4. Cereal
5. First sip of coffee
6. Acting like a kid
7. Cuddling
8. Sprawling on my bed
9. Juicing
10. Sparkles

Day 28

1. Holly plants
2. Poinsettia
3. Helping people
4. Prince
5. Belle & Sebastian
6. Sharing knowledge
7. Empowering people
8. Relaxing
9. Chocolate chip cookies
10. Ginger cookies
11. Good sparkling wine

Day 29

1. Lasagne
2. Dentist
3. My family
4. Being love

5. King-size beds
6. My life
7. Smell of puppies
8. Ice cream cones
9. Swings
10. Listening to self-help shows

Day 30

1. Rare books
2. Netflix Fridays
3. XXX
4. Technology
5. Managing archives
6. Genealogy
7. Temples/sacred sites
8. Baklava
9. XXX
10. XXX

Day 31

1. Doing a handstand
2. Lazy weekend mornings
3. Masturbating
4. Plants
5. Making people laugh
6. Ginger
7. Costume parties
8. Driving
9. Dancing
10. Fit men

Loving Kindness Meditation
33 times

Appendix II

Love Action Matrix and Checklist

Love Action Matrix

You can select any of these at any time, or do them all. This matrix is designed to provide guidance in selecting love actions that are meaningful to you, based on what is transpiring in your life.

Love Action	Self-Love	Just Love	Spread Love
Hug Yourself	X		X (if imagining others when hugging)
Meditate*	X	X	X
Heart Breath	X		
Love in the Mundane		X	
Luscious, Luxury Love Moments (LLLMs)	X		
Affirmations and Mirror Work	X		

Love Action	Self-Love	Just Love	Spread Love
Letting Go/Surrender*	X	X	X
Sending Love			X
Things I Love		X	
Loving Kindness Meditation			X

*Letting go or surrendering and meditating are both love actions that serve all three love themes shown above. For instance, with meditation, you can meditate on different subjects that can influence the love you are feeling. Or you may meditate on forgiveness for someone who wronged you; that is showing love for yourself and the person. Perhaps you meditate on healing your inner child; that is love towards yourself. Any meditation, I believe, is beneficial and therefore an act of love and will boost your vibration, so it's considered a love action for just love.

It is the same with letting go or surrendering. If you let go of an argument you had with a partner, that is showing love to that person, and they will feel it through your new attitude and energy. Or if you surrender to the outcome of a new project, you are loving yourself by not stressing about the unknown. Plus, letting go and surrendering opens your heart to possibilities, which puts you in a higher vibration and more aligned with love.

Love Action Checklist

You can use this to keep track of the love actions as you do them for any of the challenges. A version of this is also available on my website, colindalatour.com.

Love Actions/ Days	Hug Yourself	Meditate	Heart Breath	Love in the Mundane	LLLMs	Affirmations/ Mirror Work	Letting Go/ Surrender	Sending Love	Things I Love	Loving Kindness Meditation
1										
2										
3										
4										
5										

Love Actions/Days	Hug Yourself	Meditate	Heart Breath	Love in the Mundane	LLLMs	Affirmations/Mirror Work	Letting Go/Surrender	Sending Love	Things I Love	Loving Kindness Meditation
6										
7										
8										
9										
10										
11										
12										

Love Actions/ Days	Hug Yourself	Meditate	Heart Breath	Love in the Mundane	LLLMs	Affirmations/ Mirror Work	Letting Go/ Surrender	Sending Love	Things I Love	Loving Kindness Meditation
13										
14										
15										
16										
17										
18										
19										

Love Actions/ Days	Hug Yourself	Meditate	Heart Breath	Love in the Mundane	LLLMs	Affirmations/ Mirror Work	Letting Go/ Surrender	Sending Love	Things I Love	Loving Kindness Meditation
20										
21										
22										
23										
24										
25										
26										

Love Actions/ Days	Hug Yourself	Meditate	Heart Breath	Love in the Mundane	LLLMs	Affirmations/ Mirror Work	Letting Go/ Surrender	Sending Love	Things I Love	Loving Kindness Meditation
27										
28										
29										
30										
31										

CPSIA information can be obtained
at www.ICGtesting.com
Printed in the USA
LVHW041349200423
744756LV00001B/223